White Railings

Design and artwork by Paul Eaton, Galante Design
www.galantedesign.co.uk

Printed in the UK by Orphans Press
www.orphans.co.uk

ISBN: 978-0-9570248-1-6

White Railings

Recipes And Reflections From A Shropshire Mill

Ian Hankinson

Contents

About This Book

I n 1984 I moved with my wife Ann to a semi-detached converted water mill in south Shropshire. I carried on working for the Probation Service while Ann kept house and continued to develop her repertoire of recipes. As we were assimilated into the social networks of our rural community, so our circle of friends expanded. The invitations we offered to come to 'supper at the Mill' gradually became highly prized and Ann's food and wine are now locally regarded as unique treats to be savoured. When I retired in 2009 I was able to fulfill the long standing ambition to gather Ann's favourite recipes together in a book. As I did so it seemed natural to also reflect on aspects of our life together since moving to the Mill, and to identify the connections between some of these reflections and particular recipes.

This is not intended to be a book that has to be read from the beginning to the end in that order. It was written in that way and if you want to read it like that then it will, I hope, make sense. However, the various prose chapters are self-contained and can be sampled in whatever quantity and order the reader chooses. Most of the chapters connect to particular recipes, and if you want to move on from those to other similar recipes (e.g. one cake recipe might encourage you to seek out others!) then these can be found categorised in the **Mainly Recipes** section. The **Contents** page lists the prose chapters but you'll have to read a chapter to find out what recipes it connects to. If your interest is in the recipes alone, go to the **Mainly Recipes** section and at the end of each section you will find links to similar recipes that are located in the **Mainly Reflections** chapters.

White Railings?

I f like me you are or were lucky enough to know your grandmothers then I expect there are one or two memories of time spent with them, or stories told by them, that instantly bring them to your mind. I will be sixty years of age soon and both my grandmothers died many years ago, both in their nineties. Their memories stretched back to the early years of the last century. I remember both of them very well and each of them had a particular story about their lives that seems to me to chime with mine.

All the recipes in this book have been found or adapted or invented by my wife Ann (pictured above). She is ten years older than me and when we married in 1980 there was some muttering in certain quarters about the age gap between us. We discovered many years later that Ann's friends in the Gingerbread group for single parents, which she co-founded following her divorce from her first husband, all thought that 'it would never last'. We have proved them wrong and I don't think either of us ever had any serious doubts that we would. My paternal grandmother Miriam had a similar, but much more challenging experience when she married my grandfather Bert (or Bertie as she more affectionately called him throughout their marriage). She was the daughter of a prosperous builder; he was six years younger than her and merely an NCO in the Military Police having been a junior clerk in the Home Office before he volunteered in 1914. Miriam was already engaged to be married to the wealthy owner of a Malayan rubber plantation when she met Bertie in 1916 while he was on leave (and her fiancée was in Malaya). After a whirlwind romance Miriam broke off her engagement and decided to marry Bert. Both knew that Miriam's father would oppose them because Bert was too young and too poor to be considered 'suitable', and so they married in a registry office in complete secrecy. The only people who knew were the Registrar and the two witnesses, Miriam's sister and her best friend. After the ceremony Miriam returned home and continued to live as if she were an unmarried daughter in her parent's house. She put her wedding ring onto a chain which she wore around her neck, concealed under her clothes. Bert went back to the Great War, his regiment being designated as reinforcements during the Battle of the Somme and getting to within a few miles of the front line before being abruptly turned around and sent to Greece to fight on the Bulgarian front. Only when he returned from the army in 1919 were they able to declare that they were married, and begin to live together as man and wife.

Almost all of my working life was spent in the Probation Service, and it was when Ann started a second career as a Probation Officer that we met. It's over one hundred years since the first Probation Officers were appointed but it's still a role that is only partially understood by the general public. Everyone knows that Probation Officers exist but few people know exactly what they do. However, this doesn't stop anyone from having an opinion about 'what should be done' about crime and criminals. I'm sure if I tried to tell farmers what I thought was the best way to grow their crops, or pressed unsolicited financial advice on accountants I happened to meet in the pub, I would be rightly seen as being just a bit too self opinionated for my own good. No such restraint is felt when a stranger asks me what I do (did) for a living. "I was a Probation Officer", I would say. "Oh! How interesting", would be the reply, often followed not by "tell me what you think about reducing offending", but by something along the lines of "what they should do is bring back hanging/the birch/proper prison sentences. That would soon stop these hooligans/wasters/evil people committing crime". If only it were so simple. Usually the assumption is made that crime is now much worse than in the 'good old days' and that is when I like to tell people about my maternal grandmother.

In the years leading up to the First World War my grandmother Louisa and her husband ran a pub in Haggerston in the heart of the East End of London. In later life Louisa would love to tell her grandchildren tales of life on the streets of the East End in the first years of the twentieth century. One of her favourite stories was of the time a young man who she knew as a regular customer burst into the bar in panic and pleaded for her to hide him as he was being pursued by members of one of the 'razor gangs' in the neighbourhood. He was a small man and Louisa managed to hide him behind the bar counter and under her Edwardian skirts just as the gang ran in after him. Under questioning from the knife wielding leader of the gang she denied all knowledge of the man, while he crouched in terror beside her. Robberies were commonplace and Louisa and her husband slept with a revolver under their pillow as a precaution. That's what she told me anyway and I believed her.

And what has any of this got to do with this book? Well Ann is also a grandmother and it is partly at the suggestion of her grandchildren that we decided to try to put all her favourite recipes into a book. All six grandchildren have fond memories of visiting us at the Mill when they were younger and of the wonderful home cooked food they would be given while they were here. On the long journey from their home they would anticipate the meal that Grandma Ann would be cooking for them and get more and more excited until at last they would turn off the main road into the narrow lanes leading to Broncroft. When they saw the white railings just before our drive they knew they were almost there. So that's what we decided to call the book.

A Technical Note About The Recipes

All the recipes in this book are set out as Ann uses them in her day to day cooking at home. She uses an electric fan oven and finds that her oven tends to cook slower than the similar one used by her friend Liz Beazley. Readers should therefore treat the cooking times and temperatures in the recipes as guides, and be prepared to adjust them as necessary in the light of experience. As Ann has been cooking for 50 years her recipes use imperial measurements, and we have left them as they appear in Ann's recipe files. The following approximate conversions may be useful:

Weight

lb/oz	g
½	15
1	30
2	50
4 (¼lb)	110
8 (½lb)	225
1lb	450

Volume

floz	ml
1	25
5 (¼pint)	140
10 (½pint)	285
20 (1pint)	570

Oven Settings

°C	°F	Gas Mark	Description
140	275	1	very cool
150	300	2	cool
160	325	3	warm
180	350	4	moderate
190	375	5	fairly hot
200	400	6	fairly hot
220	425	7	hot
230	450	8	very hot
240	475	9	very hot

Mainly Reflections

1

In The Beginning

As with many things that seem now to have always been fundamental aspects of my life, I can't remember exactly why or when we decided that we wanted to live in the country. It's the same with Hendrix, and mild beer, and Manchester City FC: I know that there was a time when these meant nothing to me, and I know I now can't imagine life without them. But exactly when and where did that surely magical moment occur when I first tasted Bank's Mild, or heard *Purple Haze*, or watched Colin Bell? It just seems like they crept up on me when I wasn't looking and then suddenly they were there, fully formed passions that I can never relinquish.

What I do remember are Friday evenings in the Lamp Tavern in Dudley, drinking Bathams beer and talking about what our country cottage would be like if we ever managed to get there. Ann would always say that she wanted roses growing over the door, and I would promise her that one day her wish would come true. This was only one of a long list of requirements we drew up for our perfect rural retreat, but it's one of the few that we achieved. Even that was not straightforward. Essential requirement number six was that the house must face south to enable Ann to sit in the garden in the sun for the maximum possible period. In fact we face north-west. It took a bit of research and some careful nurturing before I managed to persuade a climbing rose to flourish in the chilly shade around our front door. The house is also not detached, it doesn't have a level garden amenable to vegetable growing, access is poor, it doesn't have its own drive, nor does it have a utility room. The sloping ceilings and protruding beams in the upstairs rooms are entirely unsuitable as living space for anyone over average height. I stand 6 feet 7 inches (2.01 metres for younger readers) in my bare feet. When we moved here in 1984 the house was damp, poorly maintained and insulated, with no central heating and no carpeting on the floors. There wasn't even a proper space to park the car.

And yet as soon as we saw Broncroft Mill we knew we couldn't live anywhere else. It's hard to say exactly why we fell in love so completely with the place; the tranquil setting, the babbling brook, the views of fields and hills, the sense of history in the thick stone walls and undulating roof, all these of course were part of it. But for me the trees were the thing. Old mature oak trees, plantations of young ash saplings, winding lines of riverside alders; everywhere you look there are trees. And best of all for me, our garden incorporated the edge of a small wood so that a few mature trees came within our ground. On the edge of the stream there is an old oak, twisted and gnarled and with its riverside roots undermined by the river in spate. Further away from the water, up the steep slope slippery with decades of leaf litter, is an ash that marks the corner of our ground. The rooks like to build their precarious nests right at the top of its many high branches. Between the two, and best loved by me and the rooks, is a single Scots Pine. Our bed is positioned in such a way that when we look from it through the window it frames this beautiful tree. All year round we can see its lustrous dark green head set in stark contrast with the elongated trunk. There are as many variations of wonderful deep colour in its bark as there are variations in the light; the constant changing of seasons, time and weather producing hundreds of different shades of red, orange and brown.

2

Casseroles

Our first meal at Broncroft Mill was a casserole. It had been prepared the day before the move and our neighbours kindly allowed us to heat it up in their kitchen. Being 'townies' we turned on the electric oven and waited for this to heat up, never thinking to simply put it into the already warm oven of the Rayburn. We sat in the garden on boxes eating it in the warm spring sunshine and decided that we would like it here.

Casseroles are the sort of thing that Ann tells me even I could cook. As long as you cook on a low heat in the oven nothing much can go wrong. Ann still has her Wolverhampton-made slow cooker, given to us as a wedding present more than 30 years ago, and this is brilliant for cooking casseroles. You can use any cut of meat; you simply cook the cheaper cuts for longer. As our first Broncroft meal demonstrated the best thing about them is that they can be prepared and cooked in advance. I guess this is the type of situation where many people would turn to the humble casserole. We sometimes have one if we are going out walking for the day, or visiting different towns with weekend visitors. However, Ann also uses them frequently when we are entertaining because it allows her to spend more time with our guests and less time in the kitchen. For these occasions she likes to 'jazz them up' (as she puts it) in some way. One way of doing this is by adding different vegetables, like courgettes, peppers or aubergines.The vegetables served with the casserole can also be 'tweaked' a little from the ordinary. Ratatouille is an obvious option, especially with seasonally fresh ingredients. A favourite of mine is to serve dauphinoise potatoes and with this you can even cook the potato dish in the oven with the casserole.

Gratin Dauphinoise

1 lb potatoes
2 oz butter
½ pint double cream

1 clove of garlic
Salt and pepper

This is a very rich dish with some recipes including cheese and eggs. The original French version uses only thick cream and potatoes. Pre heat the oven to 150°C and then peel the potatoes and slice them evenly and thinly. Rinse the slices in cold water and dry them with a tea towel. Take an oven proof gratin dish (the French use earthenware), rub the inside with a cut garlic clove and butter it well. Layer the potato slices in the dish, separating each layer with a sprinkling of salt and pepper. Pour the double cream over the potatoes, dot with more butter, and bake for 90 minutes. If the potatoes don't seem to be browning after 80 minutes, turn the oven up to get a golden brown crust on the top. If you want a less rich version of this dish use half milk and half cream, or even substitute yoghurt or crème fraiche for the cream.

Another interesting vegetable dish to go with casserole also came to us from France, but from my English friend Peter who has lived there ever since we both graduated in the 1970s. It's a very simple variation on the same theme but seems to add a certain richness and quality to the casserole meal.

Peter's Gratin

This is so simple it doesn't really qualify as a recipe. All you need are some tomatoes and courgettes (the exact quantities don't matter much and Ann usually just uses whatever she has in the fridge), some cheese, breadcrumbs, olive oil and seasoning. Pre heat the oven to 180°C. Slice the courgettes and tomatoes and put a layer of courgettes, and then a layer of tomatoes, in the gratin dish. Season well with salt and pepper, chopped garlic and a sprinkle of olive oil. Top off the dish with a mixture of breadcrumbs and cheese and a sprinkling of olive oil. Bake for 30 minutes.

Middle Eastern flavours can add interest to any casserole and Ann frequently turns to her Claudia Roden books for ideas in this area. Here is just one example of a really flavoursome casserole, adapted by Ann from Claudia Roden's book *Arabesque*.

Turkish Lamb Casserole With Aubergine Cream

For the casserole:
1 large chopped onion
2 tablespoons olive oil
1½ lb lean tender diced lamb
3 fresh peeled and chopped tomatoes
Salt and pepper
A small bunch of coriander

For the cream:
1½ lb aubergines
3 tablespoons butter
3 tablespoons flour
½ pint milk
¼ lb grated Gruyère cheese

Pre heat the oven to 180°C. Fry the onion in oil until soft and then add the meat to seal it. Add the tomatoes, season with salt and pepper and then add sufficient water to just cover it. Put in the oven for about 1 hour until the meat is tender. Bake the aubergines in a very hot oven (230°C) for about 30 minutes until they are tender. Leave them to cool and then peel them and squeeze out the bitter juice. Mash the flesh with a fork. Make a sauce by mixing the flour to a paste with a drop of milk. Put the remaining milk in a saucepan with the butter and bring to the boil. Now gradually add this to the flour, stirring so it does not go lumpy. Put the mixture back in the saucepan, add the aubergine puree, and cook for a few minutes. Add the grated cheese and garnish the finished dish with coriander. This sauce is very rich and tasty. Ann usually serves this dish with basmati rice but it is just as good with potatoes, or the more traditional bulgur wheat.

Ann has been a fan of Claudia Roden's books for a while, and when she first started looking for her various books they were not widely known or available. Ann's bargaining skills were demonstrated some years ago in Chester when we came across a copy of Claudia Roden's first book, *A Book of Middle Eastern Food*, in an upmarket second hand bookshop. It was not cheap, and it emerged that this was because it was a first edition. After some time Ann convinced the vendor that she was not a collector of first editions but a cook who admired Claudia Roden's work and the combination of her transparent sincerity and her stubborn persistence eventually wore the poor man down and he let her take it away for half the asking price.

Strawberry Jam

3

Jam As A Currency

We are very fortunate to be able to get wonderful lamb from our good friend Paul, who produces organic lamb on pasture just a couple of miles away from the Mill. From the study window we can just see one of his fields in the distance. It was a little while after we had met and become friends with Paul and his wife Cheryl that they realised how they had first heard about our move to the Corvedale. In those days the 'grapevine' was almost instantaneous. 'Incomers' to the Dale were still few and far between and it was taken for granted that everyone knew everyone else living within a few miles of them. I remember the realisation (perhaps 10 years ago?), that the drivers of cars passing us as we walked along our lane no longer routinely waved or stopped for a chat. In 1984 a car driven by a stranger was a topic of local conversation. And so it was that unbeknownst to us at the time, our arrival at Broncroft Mill had been extensively discussed in the hamlets and dwellings in our part of the Dale. Soon after we had moved in we had encountered Jack Jones, the local plumber, builder, grave digger and drainage expert. On the advice of our neighbours we rang him whenever we had a plumbing problem. He would arrive in his old van, engage in general conversation for half an hour, then fix the problem, usually with a piece of old piping from the back of his van. Then would come the debate over payment. "How much do we owe you Jack?" we would ask. Jack would procrastinate and dissemble and would only accept a fiver or tenner with great reluctance. We soon discovered that the way to compensate him for his time and trouble was to offer some service of ours in return, usually jars of Ann's marmalade or jam. These were valued by Jack much more highly than mere money. Anyone can have money and pay people with it. That implies nothing beyond a mere commercial transaction. Offering produce made by Ann with her own hands in exchange for Jack's time and expertise signified to him (and in due course to us) that we had made a commitment to the community we had moved into, and the unspoken obligation of neighbourly support and reciprocity that was one of its core values. Anyway, it seems that Jack had had long conversations over the garden fence with his then neighbour Cheryl about "the nice lady who's moved in at the Mill and makes lovely jam". It was only after we had become good friends that Cheryl suddenly realised that Ann was Jack's 'jam lady at the Mill'.

Years ago a neighbouring farmer grew blackcurrants and gooseberries commercially and after the harvesting machines had finished their work we would be given permission to pick what remained for free. But these days almost all of the soft fruit we use for jam making is obtained from local Pick Your Own farms. Ann particularly likes strawberry jam but this is one of the hardest of jams to get to set. Ann adds redcurrants to help when she's 'boiling for a set'.

Strawberry Jam

2lb strawberries
8oz redcurrants
1½lb sugar
1 lemon

The night before you make the jam put the strawberries, redcurrants and the sugar in a large saucepan and shake to mix them together. Next day slowly heat the fruit and sugar in the saucepan. When the sugar has dissolved add the lemon juice and turn up the heat until the jam is bubbling. After 10 minutes spoon a little jam onto a chilled saucer and put this in the fridge. Once it is cool push it with your finger; if it crinkles then it is set. If it doesn't, boil for another 5 minutes and then test again. Once you have achieved a set remove the pan from the heat and leave for 15 minutes before pouring into jars. Heat the jars in a moderate oven for 5 minutes to make sure that they are completely dry. Wait until the jam is cold before applying labels to the jars.

My favourite jam is gooseberry. This is easy to make and not commonly available in shops. This makes it an excellent 'present' to give to friends when we visit.

Gooseberry Jam

2 lb gooseberries
1¾ lb sugar
13 floz water

Top and tail the gooseberries and then put them in a pan with the water. Heat slowly at first, mashing the fruit as it softens and continue to cook until the contents of the pan are reduced by about one third. Now add the sugar, stir until dissolved, and bring to the boil. Boil briskly for about 15 minutes and then test for a 'set'. This jam usually sets easily.

Delicious though these jams are, they do require the purchase of the fruit. If we can get the fruit for free this does seem to enhance the flavour! Over the years we've tried quite a few. When the grandchildren were little, Ann would make blackberry and apple jam for them. Damson jam is also good, though stoning the damsons to start can be a tedious chore. In her more competitive younger days Ann made raspberry jam especially for the filling of her Victoria sponge entry to the local horticultural show. Through experience over several years she found that when her entry used shop bought jam it did not stand out but with her homemade jam she always won a prize.

When plums are plentiful on our neighbours' trees and our freezers have no more space for them Ann makes plum jam with the surplus. More unusually she also makes a wonderful jam out of quinces. It used to be very difficult to find commercial varieties of quince in either markets or gardens and so usually she has used the fruits from the japonica shrub (*Chaenomeles speciosa*), commonly grown for its beautiful spring show of flowers and also known as Japanese quince. In fact the recipe came from a friend who had access to quite a quantity of these and wanted to make some use of them. The fruits are small and waxy yellow, it takes a lot of effort to produce a small quantity of usable flesh, and the method used is less straightforward than that for making ordinary jam. However, the jam that results is fragrant and rich like no other.

Quince (Japonica) Marmalade

Boil enough water to cover the quinces in a large saucepan and then add your quinces. Up to 12 large quinces can be accommodated. Bring the pan to the boil again and then remove it from the heat. Once the quinces are cool peel them, cut them in half and remove the pips and the core. Now weigh the fruit and put an equal weight of sugar in a pan, cover it with water and bring to the boil. Add the quinces and simmer until you have achieved richly-coloured, thick syrup. It is very important not to stir the mixture while it is cooking.

Bottle the marmalade in warm jars. (N.B. Commercial varieties of quince are now becoming more available; we can buy them at Ludlow Farmers' Market for example. Ann has found that if you use 'proper' quinces rather than the Japonica fruits then you need to simmer them for about 15 minutes until they are soft before removing them from the heat to prepare them for peeling. The resultant jam is also much sweeter so we use less sugar and perhaps add lime juice to take the edge off this.)

Ann sent this recipe to Nigel Slater after he'd written about quinces in his Observer column. To our surprise he replied via a postcard to thank her for doing so. We thought this a generous and thoughtful act and have preserved the card for posterity. Unfortunately the ink has already faded so it is unlikely that it will provide an opening for our grandchildren to appear on any future edition of *Antiques Roadshow*. Although Nigel called it quince jam we have always called it quince marmalade. I wondered what the difference was between the two terms and consulted the *Larousse Gastronomique* cookery encyclopaedia. According to this respected source the term marmalade should now only be applied to "items prepared with citrus fruit", but it then interestingly goes on to say that "originally marmalades were made with quinces: the word is derived from the Portuguese marmelada, quinces cooked with sugar or honey". So perhaps we are both right in a way.

Marriage of

MISS DORIS HAMBRIDGE

DUDLEY

MR. R. L. KIRK

WALSALL

17TH JUNE
1939

BY APPOINTMENT

FRANK COOPER'S
"OXFORD"
HOME MADE
SEVILLE MARMALADE
WARRANTED PURE
PREPARED ONLY BY
Frank Cooper Limited
OXFORD

HIGHEST AWARDS.

ESTABLISHED 1874.

REGISTERED TRADE MARK.

4

Marmalade

Most people when they hear the word marmalade think of the orange variety and we are devoted fans of this most traditional breakfast preserve. One of the many insights we have gained from years of making and eating our own food is that most shop bought produce is over sugared. A good way to enhance the unique taste of whatever you are making is to reduce the amount of sugar added. So it is that in B & B's throughout the land we have grimaced in unison as we take our first taste of the toast and marmalade, shocked once again by the overwhelming sweetness of the manufactured preserve. The recipe we use tries to retain as much of the citric sharpness and robust texture of the oranges as possible.

Pat And Robin's Seville Marmalade

4 lb Seville oranges
2 lemons

4 pints cold water
4 lb sugar

Halve the oranges and squeeze the juice into a large container. Put the pips and the pith into a boiling cloth (i.e. a large piece of muslin or, if you can't find one, a cut down old cotton pillow case will do the trick). Slice up the orange peel. Put the juice and the sliced peel into a bowl with 4 pints of cold water and then place the tied up boiling cloth containing the pips and pith into it. Leave for 24 hours and then boil it all for 90 minutes. During this time squeeze the bag of pips and pith and stir from time to time. Leave for a further 24 hours and then remove the bag of pith and pips. Squeeze as much liquid as you can out of the bag when you do this. Now add the sugar and heat the pan gently until it has all dissolved. Then boil for 15 minutes before testing for a set. Once the marmalade has set remove the pan from the heat and wait for 15 minutes before potting it so that the peel does not rise to the top of the jars.

Ann makes enough marmalade in January, when the Seville oranges are in season, to last us the whole year. She processes ten or twelve pounds of fruit, and before we had a food processor the cutting up of the peel by hand was a wearisome task. The marmalade that results is less sweet and more thickly cut than all shop bought varieties. The closest to it that we have found is Frank Cooper marmalade. This used to be made in Oxford and there is a curious and entirely coincidental link between Ann and Frank Cooper, namely that Ann's mother, Doris, was given away at her wedding by Frank Cooper himself. The family story is that as a young woman she found work in her home Oxfordshire village of Kidlington at the Kidlington Zoo, which was owned by the well known local marmalade producer Frank Cooper. For some reason the zoo was moved from Kidlington to Dudley, where it still remains. Doris, and the elephants that she was employed to care for, moved with it. In Dudley she met Bob and they were married in 1939 just months before the war. The wedding invitation is curiously of its time with Bob referred to as 'Mr R.L.Kirk' (see photo on p30). For some reason not known to us, Doris's father did not attend the wedding, but Doris's employer, Frank Cooper, stood in his place.

Most of our marmalade is spread thickly on my breakfast toast and lovingly consumed and enjoyed. Some is given away as presents to friends, but Ann also sometimes uses it to make *Marmalade Muffins*.

Marmalade Muffins

5 oz plain flour
1 egg, beaten
¼ pint milk
2 oz melted butter
2 oz golden caster sugar

½ tablespoon baking powder
4 tablespoons marmalade
3 tablespoons demerara sugar
A pinch of salt

Pre heat the oven to 200°C. Sieve the flour, baking powder and salt into a large bowl and make a well in the mixture. Mix the egg, caster sugar, milk and butter together and pour this into the well. Fold together very lightly and then carefully stir in the marmalade. Put 12 small paper muffin cases into a muffin tin and divide the mixture between them. Sprinkle the demerara sugar over the muffins and bake for about 25 minutes until they have risen and are golden in colour.

These are especially useful for when we go on holiday and have to leave home in the early hours of the morning to drive to an airport. Once we've got there and checked in we can enjoy a breakfast of marmalade muffins while we wait in the departure lounge.

5

Soup And Its Many Uses

Like most people we collect recipes from our friends, and several of our favourites have come from one of my longest standing friends. Robin (pictured with me in 2009 on p37) is 25 years older than me and we first met when I went to London as a callow 18 year old to be a Community Service Volunteer (CSV) for a year before going on to university. I was found a bed-sit in Wandsworth and it turned out that Robin was my landlord and had an office/consulting room on the ground floor. Most young people on 'gap years' now travel round the globe so my nine months in South London doesn't really compare. Nonetheless I learnt many important lessons about life in general and people in particular and ever since then I have strongly supported the idea of young people leaving home and finding their own feet once they become adults. Perhaps the most important thing that I learnt was that age is irrelevant when it comes to relationships. Robin and I hit it off immediately despite the disparity in our ages, but perhaps aided by our similarity in height. When we went to parties people would assume we were brothers simply because we are both very tall. Thinking about it now I wonder why nobody thought we were father and son as our ages would support such an assumption. I suppose we behaved as friends and we remain so still. Robin had a cottage in Finmere in Oxfordshire that he and his then wife would visit at weekends and on a couple of occasions they took me with them. Two culinary experiences are connected with that place. It was the first time I ever ate jugged hare, and also the only time I've eaten that dish. I can't remember what it tasted like but I now value our all too infrequent glimpses of wild hares in the fields around us too much to contemplate a repeat. Many of our shooting friends will not shoot hares even when an opportunity arises to do so because of their scarcity in our part of the world.

Finmere was also where I first encountered the peculiar and unique Jerusalem artichoke. These curious plants are related to sunflowers and grow to about six feet tall with quite attractive yellow flowers. The tubers of the plant are like knobbly potatoes and it is these that are edible. At Finmere, all those years ago, Robin was actually trying to clear a bed of these plants because they do spread relentlessly and will reappear after being cleared if the smallest tuber is overlooked. The taste of the tubers is delicate and sweet and they make the most distinctive soup. We have yet to meet anyone who can identify the vegetable in the soup in a blind tasting. Although far superior in taste to baked beans or lentils, Jerusalem artichokes can have the same unfortunate effect on the digestive system. We always serve this soup at lunch and then take our guests out for a country walk so that the flatulent side effects can be harmlessly dispersed.

Artichoke Soup

1lb Jerusalem artichokes
Juice of 1 lemon
1 small sliced onion
2 sticks of chopped celery
1oz butter

2 pints chicken stock
Salt and pepper
½ pint milk
5floz double cream (optional)
Chopped parsley

Peel the artichokes (this is a little awkward as they are very knobbly!) and cut them into small chunks. Fry the artichokes, onion and celery in butter in a saucepan until they are soft. Add the stock and bring to the boil. Season, cover and simmer gently for about 20 minutes until the vegetables are tender. Blend in a liquidiser, add the milk (plus the cream if you want a richer soup) and reheat without boiling. Garnish the soup with chopped parsley. Robin tells me that there is now a new less knobbly variety of Jerusalem artichoke called Fuseau and if you can buy these it will make the peeling process much simpler.

Soups in general are good for lunch. We often have bread and cheese with them or, if we have visitors and want something a little more special, we serve soup with home made cheese scones. A good one for visitors is *Creamy*

7

Greece

At first glance it may seem strange to mention recipes originating in far flung countries in a book that is supposed to be about cooking, eating and drinking in the depths of the English countryside. I suppose it is a mark of how 'globalised' life has become that most of us now take it for granted that we will cook and eat food from all parts of the world as a matter of course. We take the view that there are aspects of life and experience and food that we value and seek and that these can be found both at home and in foreign parts. Making the links between different experiences and trying to identify and enhance the similarities adds value to both. So when I see swallows flying around the castle in the summer, I am often reminded of the time in Greece, on one of our annual holidays there, when we were fortunate enough to witness a pair of swallows feeding young in a nest just feet above our heads. The nest was built under the roof of one of the balconies of our apartment. At breakfast each morning we would be privileged observers, learning that the chicks could sense the imminent arrival of food and using their hunger cries to alert us to the sudden dive and swoop of a parent bird returning to the nest with a beak full of squirming insects. As our holiday fortnight went on the chicks grew bigger, then came out of the nest and perched on an adjacent ledge, and then just before we left they made their first flight, joining their squealing colleagues circling the buildings and gardens. Since then I have been able to imagine how the swallows that nest every year in our neighbour's outbuildings are following the same pattern even though I cannot witness it at such close hand for myself.

Holidaying in Greece has been part of our lives for many years. We've visited several of the islands but also some mainland resorts, always wanting to go somewhere that is not too hot and not too barren. The Ionian islands are favourites, especially Ithaca, but we've visited the mainland resort of Sivota in Epirus many times, and have also been to the Pelion twice. Our first visit there started in a particularly traumatic way. On landing at the military airport of Volos we had problems with the hire car waiting for us; I was too tall to drive it comfortably. This was of course 'no problem'; all we had to do was drive it to the main office in the centre of the bustling port of Volos and we could exchange it for a different model, one I knew I could drive comfortably. For those of you who have never been to Greece I should explain that any request that you make to a Greek person in any circumstances always elicits the response, 'no problem'. Do not be fooled into thinking this means that there is no problem. It doesn't. In fact it usually indicates that there is a problem in that your interlocutor doesn't know what the answer to your question is and so is saying 'no problem' in the hope that this will satisfy you for the time being. I think the logic is that by the time you find out that there still is a problem this particular person may well be somewhere else and so why should he/she waste time worrying about it now?

Anyway, by the time the arrangement to exchange the car had been agreed everyone else, including the rep, had gone and I had forgotten the directions she had given to us for finding the only civilian road out of the base. When we passed a column of a dozen tanks driving the other way I suspected that we had gone wrong and sure enough round the next turn we came to an exit, barred by a reinforced gate and guarded by two soldiers with semi automatic weapons. Stories of British birdwatchers imprisoned in filthy Greek jails for using binoculars within a kilometre of military installations immediately came to my mind. Fortunately my binoculars were still in the luggage and a combination of a waved passport and an expression (entirely genuine and uncontrived) conveying the idea that I was a stupid Englishman who had got lost and not a Turkish spy did the trick and we were waved through into the outside world. All I had to do then was drive into the narrow streets of central Volos (think central London only with Greek drivers), find the car hire office, explain the problem again (standing up next to the shortish Greek staff worked better than words), get back in the unsuitable car, follow the car driven by one of the Greek staff at 40 kph through the narrow streets to the company car pound, transfer all our luggage from the unsuitable car to the more suitable car that was stored there, follow the car driven by the Greek car hire man back to the hire office, fill in another set of paperwork for the new car, find my way out of central Volos and then continue our 35 kilometre journey to our accommodation. Of all the migraines I've had after arriving at our holiday destination the one I had that evening was the most thoroughly earned.

Arriving in Ithaca was an altogether different experience. After a flight to Cephalonia and a long and rather slow journey by coach from the airport in the south to the northernmost tip of the island, we embarked onto a small boat at Fiscardo. The leisurely trip across the sea from there to Ithaca was a magical start to the holiday. During our holidays on Ithaca we have become very fond of the largest village in the north of the island, Stavros. There is nothing very remarkable about it but it just seems a very friendly, almost cosy, place. We found a wonderfully good and unusual restaurant there called *Polyphemus*, housed in an old Ithacan mansion. The kitchen is downstairs and upstairs is a bar and toilets that on my first visit there in 2007 reminded me a bit of squats I visited in London in the 1970s.

There were battered old sofas, scrubbed pine tables, and posters of Che Guevara and Lenin on all the walls. Adding to the atmosphere were several pairs of swallows swooping in and out of the open windows to attend their nests built on the tops of wardrobes and curtain rails. Access is via a metal staircase on the outside of the building. Surrounding the house is a wonderful verdant garden and this is where we ate. On our most recent visit we found the upstairs has been tidied up a bit but the revolutionary posters are still there. The front of house is organised by a slim, blond, multilingual Swiss woman who told us that she came to the island years ago and was so enchanted by it that she stayed on and has lived there ever since. Her partner is the cook and she explained to us that the future of the restaurant was uncertain because "he is a Communist and just wants to be a fisherman". That explained the posters. The Greek Communist Party (KKE) has apparently always been well supported in Ithaca and on our last visit in 2011 we saw many KKE posters opposing the government's austerity programme. The food at *Polyphemus*, though authentically Greek, has a touch of class to it. For example they serve a delicious starter consisting of courgettes made into something like rissoles. Ann has worked hard to try to replicate it and though she will be the first to admit that there may still be one or two secret ingredients she hasn't yet identified, her version is always a great success, and talking point, when we serve it at home to guests.

Courgette Fritters

1½ lb grated courgettes
Salt and pepper
1 peeled and finely chopped garlic clove
15–20 finely chopped mint leaves
1 oz grated Parmesan cheese

1 lightly whisked egg
5 tablespoons self raising flour
8 oz grated feta cheese
Olive oil

Grate the unpeeled courgettes into a colander. Squeeze the liquid out of the courgettes with your hands (or if you prefer you can wrap them in a tea towel and wring them out that way). Put the courgettes in a bowl and add all the other ingredients, except the flour and the feta cheese. Stir in the flour which should be enough to bind the mixture thickly. Form the mixture into fritters. Heat some olive oil in a non-stick frying pan and shallow fry the fritters for about 2 minutes on each side until they are golden brown. Sprinkle grated feta cheese on top of the fritters and serve.

Greek food is very simple and therein lies its appeal. Even I can make *Greek Yoghurt And Honey* and this is as delicious as a dessert as it is eaten for breakfast on the balcony of your holiday apartment.

Greek Yoghurt And Honey

Spoon some Greek yoghurt into a dish. Using a different spoon drizzle a generous spoonful of honey, preferably Greek, over the yoghurt. Eat and enjoy. If you make this for two, one can have the yoghurt spoon and the other the honey spoon!

Even though Greek restaurants and tavernas don't have a great reputation among 'foodies' we have always liked the simplicity and domesticity of their cuisine. We like to eat Greek food in Greece (when in Rome etc…) and often we'll order simple dishes like Moussaka or Stefado. This type of dish is prepared in quantity and then left to be warmed up as required. If you eat this type of food in Greece, where it can still be 30°C at nine in the evening, you understand why it is designed to be served warm rather than hot. My favourite traditional Greek dish is *Pastitsio*. Ann makes this at home and it's nearly as good as the real thing.

Pastitsio

To serve 8:
5 tablespoons olive oil
2 large finely chopped onions
1½lb minced lamb
4floz red wine
6 large sliced ripe tomatoes
1½ tablespoons ground cinnamon
A pinch of cayenne pepper
1 tablespoon oregano

1 small handful of chopped parsley
1 teacup of grated cheese
1½lb macaroni or casarecce

For the white sauce:
2oz butter
4 tablespoons plain flour
1½ pints milk
1 teacup of grated cheese

Cook the macaroni in boiling salted water. Drain before it is completely cooked and return it to the saucepan. Add some olive oil and mix well. Now add a cupful of cheese. In a frying pan heat half the olive oil and sauté the onions for 10 minutes. Add the meat and cook until lightly brown. Add the wine and boil until the liquid is slightly reduced. Now add the tomatoes, 1 tablespoon of cinnamon and the cayenne pepper and boil again until the liquid is further reduced. Add the oregano, half the parsley, salt and pepper and simmer for 5 minutes. Now is the time to add more cinnamon, salt and pepper if you think the meat sauce needs it. Make a white sauce by putting the flour in a bowl and mixing in enough milk to make a smooth paste. Put the remaining milk in a saucepan, bring to the boil, and then slowly add it to the flour mixture, stirring well as you do so. Return the mixture to the saucepan, add the butter and stir until it thickens. Now add ¾ cup of cheese. Heat the oven to 180°C. Grease a baking dish with butter or oil. Spread layers of macaroni and meat to fill the dish, finishing off with macaroni. Cover with the white sauce and sprinkle with cheese. Bake for 40 minutes but let it cool a little before serving, perhaps accompanied by some lettuce and cucumber.

In Sivota we have spent many a happy evening dining on the harbour front, watching the sun set over the southernmost tip of Corfu, and sharing a portion of Pastitsio and a carafe of wine. Back in the UK the dish rarely tastes quite as good, but it always succeeds in evoking memories of the times we've spent in Greece, and the Greek olives we buy from Tamsin from *The Olive Press* stall on Ludlow Market (pictured right) have the same effect.

Pickled Garlic
Pot (250ml) £2.20
Tray (750ml) £6.50

Artichoke Hearts in oil
£00 per pot

Black Olive Tapenade
£2.00 per pot

Sundried Tomato Stuffed Olives
Pot (250ml) £2.10
Tray (750ml) £6.00

Dolmades
Vine Leaves Stuffed with Aromatic Rice
Six for £1.50

KALAMATA
Single Estate
Extra Virgin
Olive Oil
e 1L

Marinaded Button Mushrooms
£2.20 per pot

Gordal Olives
Tub (250ml) £2.00
Tray (750cc) £6.00

8

French

Connection

I suppose I've always thought of French food as being famously complicated and refined, though my experiences of French restaurants over the last 30 plus years suggests the opposite. Usually we've eaten a big piece of meat accompanied by some 'fries'. Of course, this may be because I've never been able to afford to go to expensive restaurants. On the other hand I have had the privilege of visiting Paris regularly over that period because my university friend Peter moved there to live soon after we graduated and has remained there ever since. He just loves Paris and over the years I've grown to love it too. His first address in Paris was on Quai de Bourbon on Ile St Louis. He wrote to invite me over to visit him, adding as an inducement that his address was one of the most prestigious in Paris and was right in the centre, meaning that he and I could explore the city on foot with the minimum of effort. When I got there I realised what he had meant. Notre Dame was 5 minutes walk, the Louvre, Le Marais, the Latin Quarter and the Pompidou Centre at Beaubourg a little more. But all these fantastic 'sights' and more were accessible via a gentle stroll. I also discovered how he managed to afford such an address on his salary as an English teacher for a language school in the city. The most accurate description of his 'apartment' would be to say that it was a large windowless cupboard, with just enough room for a bed, a tiny loo and shower cubicle, and an extremely compact kitchen. When I lay down on the floor in my sleeping bag my head touched one wall and my feet the other. No wonder we spent all our time out and about exploring the city.

Over the years Peter's circumstances and accommodation have improved and Ann and I have made many visits to stay with him and his French partner Christine. They now live in Vincennes, on the edge of Paris, and their flat overlooks the huge street market that fills the streets on several days each week. French street markets are fantastic for a lover of food. Not only is almost every imaginable type of food available, it is displayed and sold with extraordinary flair and panache. Outside Paris the markets are less extensive, but more particularly local, and when we've been on holiday with Peter and Christine we've always made a point of spending time strolling around the local markets looking for regional specialities to buy and enjoy. This can become so engrossing that it almost becomes the main activity of the day, and bears very little relationship to what we Anglo Saxons normally think of as routine food shopping. I guess most of us would approach this task in the UK by making a list, going to the supermarket, selecting what we want, paying for it and then coming home. When we are on holiday in France with French people it is very different.

Take, for example, *The Day We Went To Buy Milk*. That morning we ran out of milk for our breakfast cereals. What could be simpler than to drive down to the supermarket and buy some? So we got in the car and set off for the town. On our way there we remembered that it was market day and that the market was held in the streets adjacent to the supermarket, so we decided that we would look round the market first before going to the supermarket for the milk. After an hour and a half of delightful wandering through the narrow streets, with our senses stimulated by sights and sounds and smells from a large variety of stalls, we had bought: a joint of pork, a smoked ham, some sliced ham, a ham pie, three different types of saucisson from one stall, two more different types of saucisson from another stall, some bread, two different cheeses, two types of olive, three different types of haricot beans, some potatoes, some bananas, a tray of twelve melons sold to us at a knock down price because the market was near to finishing, a whole spit roasted chicken, and quite a number of other things that I've forgotten. Then we went to the supermarket for the milk. Unfortunately by this time it had shut for lunch. (In France all shops seem to shut for at least an hour and a half for lunch.) Undeterred we returned to the market and asked several stall holders if they sold milk or knew of any other stalls that did sell milk only to be met by stares of blank incomprehension as if it was self evidently completely absurd for anyone to imagine that milk could be bought at a market. Then we had a breakthrough: the stallholder of a cheese stall who had almost packed up to go said that he might have some. He obligingly searched in his van and produced an unlabelled litre size squash bottle full of milk. We bought it gratefully and then asked why it was not in a branded container. The answer, obvious in hindsight, was that this was local food at its best. The milk was from the stallholder's own cow, produced by his own hand that very morning. As long as we realised that it was unpasteurised, and therefore needed boiling before use, he was sure we would find it delicious on our cereal. So we returned from our shopping trip without the standard sem-skimmed milk we had had in mind to buy when we set out, but with an experience to savour. It was also during this holiday that Peter gave us the recipe for his delicious *Tarte Tatin*.

Peter's Tarte Tatin

1lb dessert apples, peeled, cored and thinly sliced
4oz soft dark brown sugar
2oz butter

1 teaspoon ground cinnamon
Shortcrust pastry (made with 4oz plain flour and 2oz butter)

Preheat the oven to 180°C. Melt the butter and sugar together and put this mixture into an 8 inch, one-piece tin. Sprinkle some cinnamon over it. Arrange the apples neatly in a circular pattern around the tin. Roll out the pastry and cut out a circle that will cover the top of the tin plus a little overhang. Lay the pastry over the apples and tuck the edges down around the edge of the tart. Place in the oven and cook for 30 to 40 minutes until the pastry is golden. Take the tart out of the oven, place a plate on top and turn it upside down. You can vary this dish by using frozen flaky or puff pastry with success. Peter's special addition is to spread commercial liquid caramel over the apples and sugar before cooking. He serves a glass of Calvados with each portion and advises that you pour some into your spoon and sprinkle it over the tart before starting to eat it.

When we come back from a visit to France we always bring back a bottle of Calvados especially for this dessert. Often this is the only alcohol we come back with: not for us the creaking springs of the over-laden car as it battles back up the motorway with too many cases of French wine stashed in the boot.

9

Making And Drinking Wine

Even before we moved to Broncroft Ann was a keen 'country' wine maker. What she calls 'bought' wine was always appreciated as a treat, but for everyday drinking our finances pointed us towards homemade alcohol. Once you buy a few books about homemade wine you quickly come to realise that you can make wine out of more or less anything. So when we first moved to the country we did. As long as the ingredients were free, and freely available, we made wine from them. For the first few years we had at least 25 different wines on the go at any one time. As with the jars of jam and marmalade we would give bottles of wine to friends and neighbours in exchange for dinner invitations or favours done. Our circle of friends expanded rapidly during this period.

Making homemade wine is quite hard work and over the years we have tried to cut down on the amounts we make. We leave wine for at least 2 years before drinking it so the process of deciding which wines we like and which we don't has been gradual. Nevertheless, after 27 years of effort, we have now got down to a short list of our favourite wines. These we make, the rest we leave to others. However we still seem to have a house full of bottles, demi johns, plastic bins and other wine-making paraphernalia. One of the reasons for this is that it turns out there are quite a few wines that we really like, and are loath to give up. Counting them up for this book I make it at least seven, namely damson, blackberry, oak leaf, dandelion, elderberry, apple and blackcurrant.

Try as we might we have not yet managed to liberate ourselves from the seasonal imperatives of the wine maker's harvest. When a particular ingredient is ready to gather then gathering it has to take priority over everything else otherwise the moment will pass and we will be left with nothing but a bitter regret over produce, in our eyes, 'gone to waste'. It is no coincidence that the wines we now confine ourselves to are all made with free ingredients. These are either gathered from the hedgerow, or harvested from the orchards and gardens of friends. Turning down the offer of free fruit is hard, and our practice of offering a sort of 'tithe' in bottles of wine from the previous year's harvest to the owners of the fruit trees only makes it harder because they are so much the keener to repeat the transaction, and we then fear the guilt not only of 'wasting' free fruit, but also of depriving friends of wine made from their very own produce. So it is

that in the autumn especially we still have periods of several days at a time when all we do is harvest and process fruit for wine.

The wine making season starts, however, in the spring, and with one of the less usual wine making ingredients. For many people the start of spring is symbolised by young lambs in the fields, the first swallows returning, daffodils on grassy banks and along the lane verges, green shoots from hawthorn hedgerows. I love and eagerly anticipate all these, but for me spring means picking dandelions from the banks of the road to Bouldon in warm spring sunshine. What for others can be a pernicious weed is for us the ingredient for a delicious, sherry-like wine, although we have never been able to identify exactly which aspect of the flavour is attributable to the dandelions themselves. We make three gallons each year and serve it as an aperitif.

Dandelion Wine

4 pints dandelion flower heads (without calyx)
1 lb raisins
2 lb 12 oz sugar

½ oz citric acid
15 drops of liquid grape tannin
Water to make up 1 gallon
Wine yeast

It is imperative that the flowers are picked on a sunny day. It is traditional to do this on St.George's Day, April 23rd. Use a bucket that has a pints scale on the inside. Pull the yellow petals away from the flower head and discard the rest. It is easier to do this as you are picking rather than waiting until you get home. Put the petals in a bin and pour over them 7½ pints of boiling water. Put on the lid and leave to soak for 2 days (and no more). Put the sugar and the raisins into the initial fermentation bin. Transfer the flower heads and liquor to a large saucepan and bring to boiling point. Then strain this into the fermentation bin and stir to dissolve the sugar. When cool add the grape tannin, citric acid, and the wine yeast. Ferment for 7 days and then siphon the liquid off the 'pulp' into a fermentation vessel. Fit air lock and ferment to a finish in the normal way, racking as necessary in due course.

Our other 'hedgerow' wine is also made in the spring. Oak leaves are an unlikely ingredient for wine but if young leaves are picked then the result is a white wine that is excellent in the summer if served well chilled. The hedgerows along our local lanes do have some oak in them and picking leaves from these, rather than from a tree, seems to give the best flavour.

Oak Leaf Wine

1 gallon oak leaves (measured in a bucket)
2¾ lb sugar

Juice of 2 lemons
Water
Yeast

Put the leaves in a bin. Bring 4 to 6 pints of water to the boil and dissolve the sugar in it. When it is clear pour it, boiling, over the leaves and leave to infuse overnight. The next day strain the liquor into a fermentation vessel, add the lemon juice and yeast and mix well. Top up with cold water if necessary and then ferment it out in a warm place. Rack it after a few months, and bottle after a year. This wine is best drunk young and well chilled

Our busiest time though is in the autumn. The wine we have always thought of as our best, and which we make and drink more of than any other, is damson. Damsons are a very underrated and neglected fruit, perhaps because they are often not readily available commercially. We are very fortunate to have a number of friends who have damson trees on their ground. Over the years they have become accustomed to our September enquiries as to the state of this year's crop and often they will contact us to offer the crop before we have spoken to them. Ann has tried several different recipes for Damson wine over the years but it always comes out well.

Damson Wine

5 lb damsons
1 gallon water
1 lemon

2¾ lb sugar
Yeast

You don't need to remove the stones from the damsons but you do need to discard the stalks. Put the damsons into a bin and pour half the boiling water over them. Let them cool and then use your hands to squeeze the fruit. Try not to leave any intact damsons (you won't succeed!). Peel the rind of the lemon thinly and add this to the bin. Add 2 pints of boiling water, cover, and leave for 3 days, stirring each day. Then strain the liquor into another bin, squeezing out as much juice as possible. Dissolve the sugar in 2 pints of water over a low heat and add to the juice. Add the juice of the lemon and the wine yeast. Transfer the liquid into a fermentation jar and leave in a warm place to ferment. After 3 months rack and taste to see if more sugar is needed. If it is add in the form of sugar syrup. Leave in the fermentation vessel for at least a year and then bottle the wine.

Damsons are susceptible to frost damage when the flowers are being pollinated in the spring and the pattern of damage will often vary very locally. It is common for one tree to have no fruit, and a tree two miles away to be laden. So we never know from one year to the next how many damsons will be available, or where they will be located. This tends to make us think that when a bumper crop is offered to us we should take full advantage and so a second spanner is thrown into the works as far as our stated ambition to cut down on wine making is concerned. In 2009, for example, there were good crops on trees in Tugford and up Rowe Lane. These two trees yielded nearly one hundred pounds of damsons. This equates to about twenty gallons of wine. It's about a week's work to process all this but we can't help but think that we need to 'take advantage' because perhaps next year there may be none.

If we have so many damsons that we can't use them all for wine, Ann makes a delicious purée from the remainder.

Damson Purée

8 oz damsons
½ cup sugar
¼ cup water

Put the damsons in a pan with the sugar and water, bring to the boil and then cook until soft. Push through a sieve to get rid of the stones and add more sugar to taste if you consider this is needed. When the purée has cooled you can stir it into a mixture of yoghurt and whipped cream or if you are feeling indulgent just thick double cream. Serve in sundae dishes or large wine glasses.

I think I could happily eat this for dessert every day for the rest of my life, so packed is it with fruity flavour. The fact that this taste can only be experienced by making it yourself makes it even more special.

10

Music

When I retired I received a number of farewell messages from colleagues along the lines of 'good luck with your future challenges'. I found this rather perplexing at first. After all, one of the main advantages of being retired is precisely the ability to avoid most of the challenges that you've faced routinely during your working life. Most days now I don't have to meet the challenge of waking up to an alarm clock, for example. Neither do I have to drive somewhere to arrive at a particular time. I could go on. What these colleagues were getting at, I eventually realised, was that I would want to do some new things in my retirement that I hadn't had time to do before. Knowing me as well as they did they were quite right. So I suppose one of my current 'challenges' is learning to play the saxophone. I've always wanted to play this instrument simply because it looks and sounds so cool. Well, when it's played properly it does. At other times it makes all sorts of weird and wonderful sounds. Playing like John Coltrane is easy, I've decided. The hard part is doing it to order, rather than in the middle of trying to play a Christmas carol. Perseverance is what is required, and that genuinely is a challenge for me now that I can do more or less whatever I want with my time.

When it comes to music I am definitely a child of the sixties. By this I mean that if it had not been for the musical revolution of that decade I would never have developed any sort of interest in music. I was not taught music at school and my parents rarely listened to music at home, either on the radio or on the record player. But we did have a radio, and when 'pop' records started to be played on it I began to listen. In the interests of full disclosure I have to admit at this point that the first single I bought was Frank Ifield's *I'll Remember You*, complete with yodelling. Happily I quickly moved on via the Beatles to the Stones and then onwards and upwards. *My Generation* by The Who was a favourite single in my miniscule collection, as was The Kinks' *Sunny Afternoon*. I was 14 or 15 years old and every month seemed to bring a new exciting musical discovery. Once I'd bought *Are You Experienced?* on its first day of release there was no going back; I was a hippy and my mission was to change the world.

Like most 15 year old hippies in 1968 my ultimate goal, and the means by which I was going to make my contribution to changing the world, was to be in a band. ('Group' had by then gone right out of fashion as the approved collective noun.) My mate Chris had the same idea and persuaded me to buy a bass guitar with the proceeds from selling my astronomical telescope, bought for me at great expense by my not very well off parents a couple of years previously. To them it must have been inexplicable that my interest in the stars had suddenly disappeared, and all the more galling that this was at the expense of trying to make 'pop' music. Listening to that 'awful row' was bad enough; now I wanted to try to reproduce it myself. Chris decided that we would be called 'Proelific', a name manufactured by adding an 'e' to the word 'prolific'. Not many people worked this out at the time. We didn't last long as a band and we never made a record but this was the start of my continuing interest in making music as well as listening to it. I progressed, if that is the right word, to a 6-string guitar and with the invaluable help of Bert Weedon's *Play In A Day*, I gradually learnt some chords. Later on, when I was at university, I sold my beautiful Hofner semi acoustic bass guitar and bought an Eko 12-string.

Over the years I've made a number of good friends through a shared love of music. I met Graham in Cannock soon after I started my career as a Probation Officer. We played together as a sort of folk duo for a few years (see photo on p65). Graham is in my eyes a 'proper' musician and has played, and continues to play, in a variety of semi professional bands. He's a Shropshire lad, born and brought up in Shrewsbury, and has a deep love of the Marches border country. Graham and his wife Annamarie were vegetarian for many years and quite a few of our vegetarian recipes have come from them. Soups and casseroles are particular favourites.

Lentil, Coconut And Lime Soup

1 small onion
2 oz butter
1 teaspoon cumin seeds
1 small hot chilli or ¼ teaspoon cayenne
  pepper
7 oz green or brown lentils

A pinch of turmeric
1½ pints of stock
½ pint coconut milk or 3 oz desiccated
  coconut made up to ½ pint by adding
  water
Juice of 1 large lime

Melt the butter in a large saucepan. Cook the onions until soft. Add the cumin seeds and chilli. Cook for a further minute and then add the lentils. Stir to coat well and then add the stock. Season this and bring to the boil and then simmer until the lentils are tender but with a little bite left to them. Add the coconut milk and the lime juice and simmer for another 5 minutes. Liquefy in a blender and serve after adding any necessary further seasoning.

Chestnut And Vegetable Hotpot

4oz dried chestnuts
8oz small onions
8oz carrots
8oz small sprouts
4oz button mushrooms
1 tablespoon oil
1 tablespoon Soy sauce
½ teaspoon mustard powder
Seasoning

For the dumplings:
2oz breadcrumbs
2oz Cheddar cheese
1 egg
1 pinch mustard powder
1 pinch paprika
Seasoning

First boil the chestnuts in 1¾ pints of water, then simmer for 45 minutes until tender. Drain and keep the stock. Peel the onions and carrots and slice them into thick rings. Clean the sprouts and wipe the mushrooms. Heat the oil in a casserole dish and fry the onions gently, turning them from time to time. Add the carrots and the mustard powder and continue cooking on a low heat for another 5 minutes. Add the soy sauce, chestnuts and a pint of the chestnut liquid. Bring to the boil and leave to simmer.

Now make the dumplings by mixing the breadcrumbs and grated cheese in a bowl. Add the beaten egg, mustard powder, paprika and seasoning and shape into balls. When the hotpot has been cooking for 20 minutes add the dumplings, mushrooms and sprouts. Season to taste and cook for a further 20 minutes. These quantities make 4 small portions with 8 small dumplings. The vegetables may be varied by for example using parsnips instead of sprouts or by adding a few small potatoes.

It was Graham who told me that one of the iconic traditional folk singers of the second half of the twentieth century, Fred Jordan, lived in the Corvedale. In the 80s I remember him singing at local village hall variety shows but it was only after his death that I discovered through Graham how revered he was in traditional English folk circles. Through judicious local enquiries I discovered where his cottage was, only to be told soon after that it had been bought up and was being extended. I thought it ought to be preserved for posterity but then I met the new owners and discovered that they are Fred Jordan's niece and her husband. They very kindly showed me and Graham around the house, and we had to admit that it had been tastefully converted and that the cramped one up one down ramshackle cottage that he had lived in all his life could not have lasted long in the twenty first century. All the farmers in the Corvedale knew Fred and when

I had asked them about him they described him as a farm labourer of the old school who sang a few songs after he'd had a few beers. His niece told us that she and her mother used to drive Fred to gigs. They would drop him off at the venue and then return later to collect him and take him home. She said that they too had little inkling of his status in traditional folk circles until, on one occasion, they stayed to see him perform and witnessed his star billing and the star struck devotees in the audience. As is often the way, now he and his like are gone there is a huge revival in interest in traditional English folk songs, particularly among young people.

Taking on the challenge of learning to play the alto saxophone has also revived my enthusiasm for playing music and after a gap of 30 years I've started playing music with other people and doing some live performances again. With Graham's advice I've acquired a fantastic Lowden guitar and after a spell with The Pombear Originals (now sadly no more), I'm currently playing and singing with Mandy as 'Mandian'. Our debut gig is pictured below .

ENTERTAINMENT SOCIET
adly presents

Adventures of
Aladdin

Diddlebury Village
Friday, March 18, 2
Saturday, March 19,

Corvedale Enter

CORVEDALE ENTERTAINMENT S

Sleeping B

(Wake Up Tracey Cha

DIDDLEBURY VILLAGE HA

April 23, 24

Curtains open 7.30 pm.

11

Treading The Boards

There is something about the act of performing that grabs people's attention. Why is it that performing artists – musicians, actors, singers – fascinate us? I suppose it must be that the act of creative expression, and the enjoyment of it, is particularly basic to the human condition. Why else would I, and tens of thousands of others, spend many hours learning to play a musical instrument to a fairly rudimentary standard when virtuoso performances are available to be listened to at the drop of a hat? We also seem to have a very strong urge to use our imaginations in creative ways. Telling stories and performing plays seems endlessly fascinating to us. We don't seem to mind at all that the basic plots or stories are few in number and that almost all the stories that have accumulated in print or on screen since the Greeks are re-workings in one way or another of these basic themes. How else to explain the popularity of 'soaps' on TV?

Until I met Ann I had never watched soaps on television. With the condescension ingrained in me by my privileged education I regarded them as trashy and superficial drama for the masses. However, it soon became very clear to me that if my relationship with Ann was going to progress anywhere I would have to make some sort of effort to share her addiction to *Coronation Street*. So I started watching it, and after a while I too became a devotee. I even persuaded my parents to watch it, and of course they too were quickly hooked. For me the attraction lay in the characterisations and as my career as a Probation Officer developed I found myself admiring more and more the skill of the writers in capturing so exactly the twists and turns of ordinary people's lives. The strong strain of humour that runs through *Coronation Street* also rang very true to me. My daily discussions with ordinary Black Country folk who had been put on Probation, or remanded for reports by the Court, were always full of humour, despite the fact that we were discussing difficult and often upsetting issues. Little did I think that much later I would have a hand in linking the humble Probation Service to the UK's favourite soap.

Before that happened I lost some interest in the programme because it seemed to me to be becoming too 'dramatic' and was moving away from its history and authenticity. So I stopped watching every episode. Incidentally, the same thing happened with me and *The Archers*. I used to listen to this programme regularly but gradually lost interest as the plots became less and less connected to real issues faced in the countryside. The other factor in trying to keep up with these regular soaps is simply the sheer amount of time t takes out of your life. When *Coronation Street* started broadcasting 5 episodes each and every week I decided that enough was enough and quite sincerely declared that I would from henceforth not bother to watch any of it.

The factor that caused me to modify this approach was becoming friends with one of the '*Corrie*' writers and his wife, who live a little way down the Dale from us. From him I learned that there are 15 writers on the programme, all of whom meet with the producers every 3 weeks to suggest story lines. The producers then decide which ones to pursue and allocate the scripts for the 12 or 15 episodes concerned to the writers they choose. Different writers have different strengths and interests. Our frienc likes to acknowledge the history of the programme and to continue to inject humour into his scripts. Like all the writers, he is also constantly having to think up new story lines for the characters. I don't know that this is true, but I like to claim credit for the fact that the Probation Service made a brief appearance in *Coronation Street* through Becky's rehabilitation. Fans of '*Corrie*' may remember the encounter between Hayley and Becky, after the latter had been prosecuted for stealing from the former. Hayley was horrified to bump in to Becky at college but Becky pursued her into the street to try to convince her that she was now a changed person, thanks to the intervention of her Probation Officer, who, she explained to Hayley, was called Ian. I rest my case.

In another episode of the Street written by our friend there was a scene in the hairdressers when Audrey's then admirer called in unexpectedly to talk to her. Audrey takes him into the back for a private chat, asking Maria as she does so to 'finish off with Mrs Hankinson please'. People who saw this rang us up and said they assumed that our writer friend had inserted this reference deliberately and that this was obviously very flattering......but that the customer in the salon didn't look much like Ann! How do people think these programmes are made? Do they think that the producer will ring up the writer and say "you'll have to change the name of the anonymous non speaking character called Mrs Hankinson in the salon scene because we can't find an actress that looks sufficiently like the real Mrs Hankinson"? Perhaps it is testament to the authenticity of the programme that viewers' suspension of disbelief is so total.

We've had some lovely recipes from our *'Corrie'* friends. Ann has adapted a cheesecake recipe we first had from them and uses it regularly.

Annie's Cheesecake

For the base:
5oz oat biscuits (e.g. Hobnobs)
2oz melted butter
A handful of hazelnuts (optional)

For the topping:
3oz caster sugar

8floz double cream
7oz mascarpone
7oz crème fraiche
A teaspoon of vanilla essence
12oz raspberries (but use any fruit or combination of fruits that you wish; e.g. dried apricots are good)

Process the biscuits (and hazelnuts if used) into crumbs and then add the melted butter. Mix together and press into an 8 inch loose based cake tin. Put this in the fridge to chill. Whisk the double cream until it thickens, then add the mascarpone, crème fraiche, vanilla essence and caster sugar, and whisk until thoroughly combined. Spread this mixture over the base and put in the fridge to chill for at least a couple of hours. Either arrange the fruit on top of the cheesecake before serving or simply serve in a separate dish.

One of the criticisms of soap operas like *Coronation Street* is that they trap their audiences at home in front of the telly. 'Why don't people go out to live theatre anymore?' is the complaint. Well in the Corvedale they do,

only it is a very amateur version that I and my fellow thespians try to put on at Diddlebury Village Hall each year. My mother was a keen amateur actress all her life and as a child I had some limited experience of amateur dramatics. I didn't put this to any use until about twelve years ago when I was recruited to the *Stanton Lacy Variety Show*. Sadly this wonderful annual event has recently stopped being produced but in its heyday it consisted of a whole range of different variety 'turns', sketches, songs, music, approximate reproductions of TV shows, all meshed together by Dick the compere. Everyone who wanted to 'do a turn' was able to take part so the quality of the items varied enormously. Nonetheless it enabled a whole generation of children to experience stage performance as both performers and audience. The last 'act' was always a twenty minute pantomime, and it was this that I took part in. Dick always wrote it and there were of course many local references and adaptations of the plot of whichever traditional panto he had chosen as his theme. As I can sing after a fashion I always sang a song at some point in the proceedings. The writing was incredibly inventive. My favourite was the year we did *Jack and the Beanstalk*. That year we had two other very tall middle aged men as well as me and so Dick cast the three of us as genetically modified mice. Three very small very young children in mouse costume came on at the start, one dressed in white, one in black and one in pink. Jack then got duped into selling his cow to the man from Monsanto in exchange for a bag of genetically modified beans. His Mum bawled him out, the beans were scattered, the little mice came on and ate them, the lights blacked out…and there were we three tall men dressed one in white, one in black and one in pink with mouse masks on our faces. Our roles were a pastiche of *Reservoir Dogs*; I was Mr Black as I recall.

When the Stanton Lacy Show stopped there was a demand from many local people for us to carry on putting on a pantomime and so over the last few years we have done this at Diddlebury Village Hall. I've somehow inherited the role of writer, only now it is a 90 minute show. We all have great fun doing the show but it is at a basic level of theatrical skill in every respect. For reasons that I don't fully understand this seems to make no difference at all to the enjoyment of the audience, who almost seem to revel in the inevitable unintentional mistakes. It is certainly nothing like watching a show on telly at home. Perhaps that is the root of its genuine, and to me slightly baffling, popularity.

12

Ireland

The most memorable theatrical experience of my life so far occurred in Sligo, in Ireland. We were staying in a restaurant with rooms in a nearby village and had seen advertisements for the Blue Raincoat Theatre, apparently located in an old abattoir that was being converted for theatrical use. They were presenting a play based on *Alice in Wonderland*, which sounded like fun. On arrival at the venue, which was located in a back street next to a car repair business, we were given coffee, and then at the appointed time were led into a darkened performance space and helped to our seats by staff with torches. The lights went up to reveal a stage on which were two or three large boxes; and then for the next hour and a half a succession of different Lewis Carroll characters emerged from the boxes and performed a series of scenes from the Alice books with rapier sharp wit and tremendous physicality. The whole experience was spellbinding, and also somehow to be expected in Ireland. Whereas in England the show may have been dismissed as peripheral and esoteric, in Ireland its delight in the use of language to tell mysterious and fantastical stories was very much in the mainstream.

Over the years we have visited Ireland many times and I have grown to be fascinated with its history and its many faceted culture and way of life. We first visited in 1991 when Dublin was the European City of Culture. On that visit I discovered that Irish Guinness really does taste different (and far superior) to its English cousin, and that though the words used by English speaking Irish men and women are familiar, the sentences that are constructed with them can be entirely foreign to our ears. I was also reminded right from the beginning that violence is never far away in that most serene looking but blood soaked island. On arrival at Dublin airport we took a taxi to the city and I was intrigued to see that in the driver's door pocket was a large cosh or truncheon. On enquiry the taxi driver was not in the least embarrassed and was happy to recount several recent incidents where he had used the weapon to extract money from passengers trying to avoid paying. That year of our first visit was the 75th anniversary of the Easter Rising and in the GPO building, which was the headquarters of the rebels and the scene of Patrick Pearse's proclamation of an Irish Republic, a detailed exhibition was dedicated to a glorification of that romantically doomed enterprise. Ever since then groups of Irishmen and women have claimed to be the true heirs of that tradition and have argued that it legitimises the use of force to attain political ends. Hence the continual splits in the IRA throughout its history as pragmatists accommodate to political reality and the 'irreconcilables' split to continue 'the armed struggle'. We saw plenty of street art supporting the various versions of this in Belfast in 1996 (as well as disorienting uses of the Union Jack to support loyalist paramilitary groups; the red, white and blue kerbstones in Bushmills, County Antrim, being an example that will always stick in my mind).

We went to Northern Ireland, or the north of Ireland, or 'the North' (even the phrases used to describe the country, or province, of Ulster, or

the 'six counties' are loaded with political significance) just as the 'peace process' was beginning to have an effect. The militarised border crossings were still there, but unmanned. We noticed that the police on the streets of Coleraine carried only side arms whereas those in Armagh City, nearer to the border areas, still patrolled carrying sub machine guns. Ironically my most direct and alarming experience of Irishmen carrying guns occurred in Kilkenny, in the Republic. I was waiting on a street for Ann to emerge from a shop, which happened to be next to a bank. Suddenly a convoy of vehicles roared down the street and screeched to a halt right next to me. The main vehicle was an armoured cash delivery van, escorted front and rear by Irish Army Land Rovers which positioned themselves either side of the van in such a way as to block the street from both directions. Three or four soldiers armed with sub machine guns leapt out of the Land Rovers and stood on the street and pavement covering the surrounding buildings, one stationing himself only feet away from where I stood (by this time rooted to the spot), while the security guards hurriedly entered the bank to collect the cash bags. As soon as they were back in the van, the soldiers ran back to their vehicles and with sirens blaring they roared away. Irish friends later told me that this procedure was standard practice in the Republic in the nineties because of the regular hijacking of security cash vehicles by the Provisional IRA to provide funds for 'the cause'.

As you would expect we have had numerous memorable encounters with Irish food during our visits there. I remember sitting in a restaurant in Kinsale, County Cork, and watching through the window as a funeral procession wound its way through the narrow streets, the coffin carried shoulder high at the head of the mourners. In Dublin we visited a restaurant in Temple Bar serving Irish specialities, mainly boxty pancakes as I recall, and were told that all the tables were full. Rather than being turned away it was suggested we could go into the pub directly opposite and wait to be called when a table became available. This we did, and observed several couples or groups being summoned from the very busy and (this was the 1990s) very smoky bar by the waitresses from across the road before at last, and several pints of Guinness to the good, our turn came round. Wild salmon in a tiny restaurant in Clifden, County Galway, was the finest fish I have ever eaten. A huge slab of smoked haddock, topped with a poached egg, was the best breakfast I ever had in Ireland, this being at a guest house in Cork City famed for its breakfast menu. Running this close though was the smoked salmon and scrambled egg I ate every morning during our short stay in a farmhouse bed and breakfast establishment in County Carlow. The food was good, but sitting at a vast Georgian mahogany dining table to eat it is what makes it especially memorable. And there are many more similar culinary experiences that I could describe.

The delight of freshly baked bread and scones laid out on a breakfast table is one we have encountered several times on our Irish travels. In the far west of County Cork we were offered about six different varieties by Violet Connell at her award winning Bed and Breakfast establishment. But back in the nineties we spent a wonderful week staying in a restaurant with rooms in Collooney, near Sligo, run by my cousin Katie's Irish friend, Brid. It was here that Ann was seized by her enduring passion for freshly baked scones. She particularly liked the sweet scones that they baked every morning and has evolved her own recipe for them.

Ann's Irish Scones

8 oz self raising flour
1 teaspoon baking powder
2 oz butter or soft margarine

1 egg
2 tablespoons yoghurt
A pinch of salt

Preheat the oven to 220°C. Sieve the flour and the baking powder into a mixing bowl and add a pinch of salt. Rub the butter or margarine into the mixture until it has the consistency of fine breadcrumbs. Mix the yoghurt and egg together and gradually stir them into the mixing bowl until a soft dough is formed. Roll the dough out and use a 2½ inch cutter to make approximately 8 scones. Put the scones on a baking tray and brush them with milk. Bake for 11 minutes. Serve with butter and jam (homemade of course!). Ann generally chooses strawberry jam.

There are of course many different ways to make scones. Some recipes omit the egg; some use butter, some use margarine; some use buttermilk, or even sour milk (made by souring fresh milk with lemon juice – see the recipe for *Soda Bread* on the following page).

As an aside, it was during our stay with Brid in County Sligo that we explored Lough Gill and came across the landing stage from where a boat can cross to the small island immortalised in W.B.Yeat's poem as *The Lake Isle Of Innisfree*. A collie dog appeared from nowhere and walked calmly by

Ann's side to the end of the pier. The photograph I took of them (see p76) captures something of the inner tranquility evoked for me by the poem itself:

I will arise and go now, for always night and day
I hear lake water lapping with low sounds by the shore;
While I stand on the roadway, or on the pavements grey,
I hear it in the deep heart's core.

Tastes can evoke places as well and for us the quintessential taste of Ireland is soda bread. There are, again, dozens of different recipes for this. Here is Ann's version.

Soda Bread

8oz white flour
1 teaspoon salt
1 teaspoon bicarbonate of soda
½ teaspoon cream of tartar

½oz butter
¼ pint milk
Juice of ¼ lemon
2 teaspoons yoghurt

Preheat the oven to 220°C. Add the lemon juice to the milk and leave to stand in a warm place for 10 minutes. Sieve the flour, salt, bicarbonate of soda and cream of tartar into a basin and rub in the butter. Make a well in the centre of the mixture and mix in enough of the yoghurt and soured milk to make a soft dough. Turn onto a lightly floured surface and shape into a round loaf. Place on a baking sheet and score a cross into the top with a knife. Bake for 15 minutes at 220°C and then turn the oven down to 190°C and bake for a further 8 minutes. Tap the base of the loaf to check that it is done (it should sound hollow).

One recipe that we gleaned in person in Ireland is Mrs Geary's recipe for *Chocolate Truffles*.

Mrs Geary's Chocolate Truffles

6oz cake crumbs
3oz sugar
Juice and rind of an orange

4 tablespoons apricot jam
Cooking chocolate or chocolate vermicelli

Combine all the ingredients together (other than the chocolate) and then using your hands divide the mixture into truffle size balls. Melt the chocolate and dip the truffles in it to coat them, or alternatively, roll the truffles in chocolate vermicelli.

We ate the truffles, and immediately asked for the recipe, when we collected the key for the Geary's holiday bungalow in Cloghy, on the Ards peninsula in County Down. The holiday was enjoyable, despite our problems in lighting a fire to keep warm, due, it was later found, to jackdaws nesting in the chimney. But the main thing I remember (apart from the scrawled graffiti opposite the bungalow entreating us to "remember the Somme") is the chocolate truffles!

13

Family

I fall into that increasingly large section of the population who do not have/live in a 'conventional' family structure. Ann is ten years older than me and when we were married in 1980 it was a case of 'love me…and my dog…and my two teenage daughters'. I've tried my best to do that and both my step-daughters, together with their families, have been regular visitors to the Mill. Sandra (on the left) and Sue are pictured on p84. Ann has six grandchildren, the two oldest both born in 1984. The oldest of them now has a son (Isaac pictured left with me) so for the last 2 years Ann has been a *Great* Grandma! In 1984 Ann definitely was a glamorous granny and I revelled in revealing this fact in company and watching the uncomprehending expressions as people tried to work out how this was biologically possible. My feelings on becoming a step-grandfather at the age of 30 were more equivocal, mainly because I didn't think that the term 'grandfather' could possibly be plausible when applied to me. My step-daughters thought this too, and after some discussion we agreed that their children would simply call me 'Ian'. The name 'Uncle Ian' was strongly favoured for quite some time by one of them but I couldn't bring myself to accept this term which for me has general connotations of rather perverse creepiness, as well as triggering specific memories of my time as an 18 year old working in a London children's home where the children were obliged to call the staff 'uncle' or 'auntie' and were chastised, occasionally physically, if they did not do so.

As my step-grandchildren grew older so they, one by one, began to visit us, sometimes staying over. I think they probably all have fond memories of their visits to the country and for quite a time it became the norm for one or two of them to come to stay for a week in August. During these visits Ann would try to involve them in preparing food, with the old standby of 'let's make a cake' often being invoked. Like all children they went through a 'faddy' stage but on the whole they liked what they were given to eat here and they certainly all internalised the opinion that 'Grandma Ann' knows everything there is to know about cooking. Now that they are all adults they sometimes ask for advice and Ann is pleased to give this. This of course is just as it should be. The latest request that I recall was from a granddaughter newly away at university. "How do you cook rice so it doesn't stick?" This is what Ann told her.

Easy Boiled Rice

The formula is to use double the amount of boiling water to rice. So, for example, 4oz rice would need 8floz of water. Put a small knob of butter in a saucepan and let it melt. Then add the rice and coat it thoroughly with the butter. Boil the water in a kettle and add this, together with salt to taste. Bring back to the boil, stir once, and then put the lid on and leave it untouched for about 15 minutes. Turn the heat off and leave for a further 5 minutes, then fork the rice through thoroughly and serve.

Some of the grandchildren also have favourite 'Grandma Ann' recipes that they request whenever we meet up. One is for treacle tart which

personally I always find rather cloying but which several members of the family regard as their 'greatest pudding of all time'.

Treacle Tart

6oz self raising flour
1oz corn flour
3oz soft butter
Grated rind of half a lemon
1oz caster sugar
1 large egg

For the filling:
8 tablespoons golden syrup
2oz soft butter
4 tablespoons double cream
Grated rind of 1 lemon and 1 orange
2 beaten medium eggs
4oz fresh breadcrumbs

Preheat the oven to 160°C. Sieve the flour into a bowl, and add the butter in lumps. Rub in the butter until the mixture resembles breadcrumbs in consistency. Add the lemon rind and sugar and mix. Beat the egg, mix in and bring the mixture together to make a ball of pastry. Line a greased flan tin with the pastry, cover with tin foil and line with beans. Chill in the fridge. Put in the oven and bake blind for 35 minutes. Remove the foil and check the pastry. If it is not cooked return to the oven for a further 5 minutes. Remove from the oven and allow to cool. Preheat the oven to 180°C. Mix the warmed syrup with the other ingredients and pour into the baked pastry case. Bake for 30 minutes. Remove from the oven, cover with foil, and leave for a further 15 minutes. Serve warm, ideally with custard.

My eldest step-daughter visits us more frequently than her sister as she lives much closer. Like most mothers, Ann strives to make everything perfect whenever she comes and of course this includes providing lovely food. As Sandra is vegetarian Ann has had to search out interesting and varied vegetarian recipes in order to make the meals we share special and one, in particular, has become a favourite with all of us, omnivores like me included.

Cheddar Cheese And Onion Pie

To serve 6:
For the shortcrust pastry:
12 oz plain flour
3½ oz butter
2½ oz margarine

For the filling:
1 oz butter
1 large onion, finely chopped

10 oz of grated strong Cheddar cheese
**   (e.g. Snowdonia)**
4 oz potatoes boiled and diced
2 large eggs
4 tablespoons double cream
Chopped thyme or parsley
A pinch of Cayenne pepper
Salt and pepper
A beaten egg for glaze

Sift the flour and a pinch of salt into a food processor, then add the butter in smallish pieces. Process for about 20–30 seconds and then add 2 tablespoons of cold water through the top, a tablespoon at a time, with the machine running. If the paste is still a bit dry add another tablespoon of water. Take the pastry out of the processor, wrap it in cling film, and leave it to rest for 30 minutes. Preheat the oven to 220°C. Divide the pastry into 2 balls, one a little larger than the other. Melt the butter in a pan and gently fry the onion for a few minutes. Put the onions into a bowl with the grated cheese, potatoes, eggs, cream, herbs and seasoning, and mix thoroughly. Roll out the larger of the two pastry balls and line a shallow, greased 10 inch tart tin. Put the cheese and onion mixture into the pastry case. Moisten the edges of the pastry and cover with the rolled out smaller pastry ball, sealing the edges together carefully. Brush the beaten egg over the top and bake for 30 minutes until golden brown. Because this pie is so wonderfully rich, you don't need to serve potatoes with it. We eat it with just a green vegetable such as broccoli or green beans.

Some years ago another vegetarian pie became a great favourite of one of the granddaughters who was going through a vegetarian 'phase'. This recipe was allegedly devised by the housekeeper of that famous proselytising vegetarian George Bernard Shaw.

George Bernard Shaw's Cheese And Celery Pie

For the pastry:
6oz plain white flour
1½oz margarine
1½oz Trex
Pinch of salt

For the filling:
4oz Cheddar cheese

2 stalks of celery
½ onion
2 tablespoons of finely cut green pepper
1 egg
¼ pint milk
Celery salt
Garlic salt
Pepper

Sieve the flour and salt into a bowl. Rub in the margarine and Trex until it has the consistency of breadcrumbs. Add water gradually to bind the mixture. Roll out half the pastry and line a pie dish with it.
Preheat the oven to 230°C. Finely chop the cheese, celery and onion and add the sliced pepper. Beat the egg, milk and seasoning together and combine with the vegetables. Place the mixture in the pie case and cover this with the other rolled out part of the pastry. Seal the edges well and slit the top. Brush with milk and cook in the oven for 25 minutes or until well browned.

When my parents (pictured on p84) were able to visit us, often for Sunday lunch, we generally stuck to traditional roast dinners. In our time at the Mill we have been very fortunate in our access to local meat. When we first came here we even had a butcher, based in a nearby village, who would deliver to the door. We would return from a trip to Ludlow laden with shopping to find two pork chops and a pound of mince in a plastic bag hung on our door handle. Inevitably his business failed to prosper in the face of supermarket competition, but happily Ludlow is one of the few small towns that still has some traditional butchers' shops. Until recently we had little need of them because we obtained our beef and our lamb directly from friends in the Corvedale. Sadly, they have decided to give up supplying meat directly from farm to customer, largely due to the bureaucratic impediments they faced as very small scale meat producers. So we now buy rare breed beef and lamb from Walls butchers in Ludlow. In recent years the local food movement has become more organised, commercialised and popular and there are several 'food centres' within our reach that celebrate local produce. I suppose I'm pleased by this trend but I can't help having a small feeling of disquiet that this is just a different, and currently politically encouraged, way of packaging and promoting food. The middle class customers who can afford to patronise these places on a regular basis are not really very much more connected to the people who actually produce the food than if they had shopped at one of the more ethically minded supermarkets. On the other hand we were very lucky to be able to get meat more or less directly from farmers who have produced it for many years, and clearly most people cannot do this. Maybe if we had a Waitrose on our doorstep we would be happy to shop there. We would certainly be happy to buy their eggs because we currently get our eggs directly from a farm that supplies Waitrose. We get all the rejects, (in other words they vary in size) and pay half the price. I reckon it's a good deal.

There is one family connected recipe that is not so connected with happy times. A few years ago my younger step-daughter Sue became seriously ill and during her lengthy period of treatment she became a great fan of Ann's chicken soup.

Chicken Soup

1 large chicken
1 quartered onion
2 sliced carrots
1 sliced leek

2 chopped stalks of celery
Salt and pepper
2 bay leaves
1 chicken stock cube

Put the chicken and bay leaves in a large pan and cover with water. Bring to the boil then add the vegetables and seasoning. Cover the pan and simmer on a very low heat. After an hour lift out the chicken and the vegetables and remove the meat from the carcass. Return the bones to the pan, add the stock cube, and continue simmering for another hour. Strain the broth from the bones and add the vegetables and some of the chicken. If you think it might need a little more flavour you can add another chicken stock cube. Warm this through and then serve. The remaining chicken can be used for another meal.

Ann adapted this recipe from one that her Auntie Hilda used when she was making the most of the carcass of the Christmas turkey. It makes a simple and very nourishing soup that is sometimes called 'Jewish penicillin' because it has long been considered to have medicinal properties. It certainly helped Sue in her recovery from debilitating treatment, and it is always the first proper food that any of us eat after a bout of illness to set us up on the road to recovery.

14

Golf

It was my paternal grandfather who introduced me to the game of golf, which is of course the greatest game there is. (Non-golfers might like to stop here and move to a different chapter.) I started by caddying for him on Saturday mornings when he had a regular four ball on our local (municipal) course. From him I first learned about the etiquette of the game, and its importance. Don't move or make a noise when someone is about to make a stroke; keep up a good pace and don't hold people up; call the next group through if you have to look for a ball; acknowledge your opponents' good shots and don't gloat over your own; control your frustration and temper and don't swear or throw clubs around if things aren't going well; shake hands with your opponent at the end of the game and share a drink with him in the bar afterwards. The values behind these golf specific precepts can easily translate into real life: the great golf correspondent Henry Longhurst once remarked that "the more I see of golf, the more it reminds me of life. Or, rather, the more I see of life, the more it reminds me of golf".

When I was a young teenager my interest in golf was fuelled by watching a BBC 2 series hosted by Henry Longhurst in which an American golfer played a match against a British golfer on one of the UK's premier courses. This was in the 1960s, long before the great expansion of new 'championship' courses, and so each week the viewer was given a guided tour of one of the great traditional courses by probably the most acute commentator on the game there has ever been. The actual golf match sometimes became almost incidental. I can remember nothing about the match that was played at Royal St. David's at Harlech, not even the names of the two golf 'stars' who played the match, but I vividly remember Henry Longhurst's lengthy explanation of how in years gone by the Club employed a Head Greenkeeper who had a particularly bad alcohol problem and who would walk back from the pub each night on a set route across the course. After complaints from members a local rule was introduced, applying only to the holes he crossed on his route home. On those sadly frequent occasions when the alcoholic greenkeeper had failed to make it home the night before the player was allowed a free drop if his ball ended up on the fairway within two club lengths of the greenkeeper's recumbent form. I have no idea whether this is true or apocryphal but either way it makes the point that in almost all circumstances golf, like life, must go on.

Golf and fine dining don't go together very easily. There is though the phenomenon of the golfer's breakfast. Generally this means a huge, and unhealthy, fry up. My version is confined to bacon and egg.

Ian's Bacon And Egg

2 eggs
2 rashers of smoked bacon
2 slices of wholemeal bread

Butter
Pepper
Sunflower oil

Heat some oil in a frying pan at maximum temperature and add the rashers of bacon. When they've been loudly sizzling for 30 seconds or so turn the heat down to medium, turn over the rashers of bacon, and add the eggs. Now toast and butter the bread. When the eggs have cooked to your liking, remove from the heat, put each rasher of bacon on top of a slice of toast and each egg on top of a rasher of bacon. Grind a generous serving of pepper over each egg and serve, preferably accompanied by a cup of tea.

Anyone who plays golf will know that you get good breaks from bad shots and bad breaks from good shots but that you have to simply accept these chance occurrences and get on with the game. You also, always, have to 'play the ball as it lies'; in other words, deal with the situation as you find it in the best way you can and don't distract yourself by trying to blame others or bend the rules to try to get an unfair advantage. There are of course some golfers who cheat and behave badly on the course, but they are really cheating themselves, and generally they are despised by the vast majority who do play by the rules. If your sport of choice is not golf, but perhaps football or tennis or rugby, you might like at this point to imagine in what ways your sport would change if these values were to be adopted.

I haven't even mentioned yet that in golf, uniquely I think among sports, it is the player himself who applies the rules to his play, and informs his opponents immediately he becomes aware that he might have committed an infringement of them. Try this one out on penalty 'shouts' in football. "Did I trip you there, because if I did it's a penalty to you?" "No I think I actually tripped over my own feet and anyway you got the ball so it's a corner to me, but as I tried to claim a penalty wrongly I'm going to award a yellow card against myself". If you watch golf on television and are confused by the fact that sometimes the players call for the referee, don't be; all that's happening is that the players have decided how they think the rules should be applied to themselves but are asking for a second opinion to make sure they've got it right before they carry on with the game. Most amateur golfers of course don't have this option so what they do instead is ask the Competitions Committee for a ruling; and if the Competitions Committee aren't sure, they write to the Royal and Ancient Golf Club of St Andrews, who make the rules, and ask them. Each year the R & A publish a book of *Decisions on the Rules of Golf* and for a pedantic mind like mine this is full of interest. Here's an example to give you a flavour: 'Question: What is the status of saliva? Answer: In equity (Rule 1–4), saliva may be treated as either an abnormal ground condition (Rule 25–1) or a loose impediment (Rule 23–1), at the option of the player.' See what I mean?

A common misconception about playing golf is that it must be fairly easy because the ball doesn't move as you are hitting it, unlike tennis or cricket for example. In fact it is much more challenging to hit a stationary ball. The reason is that you have time to think, and once you start thinking all sorts of contradictory imperatives fill your mind, so that when you finally come to execute the shot you are probably trying to do four or five things simultaneously. The pundits reckon that eighty percent of the game takes place between the ears. All the thousands of complex detailed sentences written about golf swings generally boil down to a few simple ideas along the lines of concentrate on what you know works, keep it simple, practise the stroke and then try to replicate it with the ball, decide on what you're trying to do and then commit to the shot. Once again, not a bad set of principles for dealing with life in general.

15

Social Networking

When it comes to technology I tend to be a bit of a Luddite. This is not because I have anything against new technology per se, it is simply that I need to be convinced that something new will actually be useful for me to use, rather than just 'the latest thing'. So although we have a computer, (and we're even now on broadband), I do not have a Facebook profile and don't use any of the social networking sites. Part of the reason for this is that our life in the Corvedale has always involved a great deal of social networking, and we don't need computers to do it. One of the most common observations about the differences between urban and rural living is that one can live in an urban street for ten years and not know any of the neighbours, but live in the country and you rapidly become well acquainted with people living in your 'patch', but miles away from you. There is almost an inverse relationship between physical and social proximity; the more scattered the population the closer the social links become. This is certainly the case in the Corvedale, which is in English terms at least extremely rural and sparsely populated. The predominant settlement pattern is one of scattered hamlets and homesteads with only a few villages, and these consist of far fewer than one hundred dwellings, the equivalent of a tiny hamlet in say Bedfordshire. And yet there are myriad social networks connecting people across the Dale, intersecting with each other in complex ways, and by doing so continually expanding the scope of any one person's 'Corvedale friends'. After living here for a while it can become difficult to remember how exactly you got to know a particular person: was it at cricket; or via the art class; perhaps they came on one of the organised walks; or did we talk to them at the church fête; or the autumn show; or were we introduced to them via another friend at one or other of these events? We met Ann's Greek teacher, Tamsin, at a party given by a man who was a friend of the man who directed the pantomime at the village hall that a friend of ours had introduced me to. This friend had been brought to our badminton club by another friend who I originally met while playing cricket for the local team after meeting the captain in the local pub and striking up a conversation. Thus does one thing definitely lead to another in this part of the world.

Our enthusiastic involvement in these interlocking networks of socialising events, which is one of the main reasons we love living here so much, has naturally featured food and drink in abundance. When we have people round to eat with us Ann keeps a record of what she has served so she can avoid any repetition when they come again. Generally our guests are happy to eat whatever they are given, and of course if they are farmers they will usually eat everything they are given as well as seconds. We did once have a visit from two Romanian teachers who were visiting my teacher step-daughter on an exchange visit. She brought them to visit us to give them a glimpse of the English countryside and so Ann prepared a traditional English meal of roast beef with all the trimmings. They ate the beef with gusto, but wouldn't eat either the gravy or the potatoes. We never really found out why. What I will never forget about their visit was the reluctance of these two, intelligent, multilingual professional women to say anything about past or present political circumstances in their home country. The shadow of Ceausescu, dead for several years by then, clearly still hung over them like a pall. I had the same sort of experience in Greece in the early eighties when I tried to discuss Greek politics with a tour guide. At the time I was bemused but I now realise that folk memories of the Civil War, and real memories of the Colonels' authoritarian military rule, still inhibited open discussion of political differences with anyone outside a person's intimate circle. I sometimes think that in this country we take these freedoms too much for granted and fail to sufficiently appreciate their significance.

Many of the recipes in this book have been served at dinner parties at the Mill. We've had lots of these, for from four to eight people, but very few bigger parties. The layout and size of our house means that it can't really accommodate more than a dozen people comfortably. So those few parties that we have given have been summer ones, with the idea that most people will be happy to eat and drink outside in the garden. We wanted to have one in the summer of 2009, to celebrate our 25 years at the Mill, but the weather was (again) so unpredictable that we hesitated to organise it in advance. In the end we had a settled spell at the end of August and at short notice we got 30 or so people to come to us on a Sunday afternoon. It was a great day and as usual Ann's food, in buffet format this time, was much appreciated. Two dishes that she uses regularly were particular favourites at that event.

Smoked Mackerel Paté

2 medium sized smoked mackerel
5 floz yoghurt
5 floz crème fraiche

Lemon juice
Pepper

Pull the skin from the mackerel and flake the fish. Mix the flaked mackerel with the crème fraiche and yoghurt. Season to taste with the lemon juice and pepper. Sprinkle with chopped chives or parsley if you wish.

Rich Three Cheese Pie

3 oz butter
6 oz white plain flour
A pinch of paprika
Salt and pepper
3 oz mature Cheddar cheese, grated
3 separated eggs

10 floz single cream
2 level teaspoons Dijon mustard
5 oz Gruyère cheese, grated
3 oz feta cheese, crumbled
4 oz Brie cheese
Pine nuts

Sift the flour, paprika and salt into a bowl. Rub in the butter, stir in the cheddar cheese and bind with 3 tablespoons of water. Chill for 30 minutes. Roll out the dough to line a 9 inch flan tin, prick the base, and chill for a further 30 minutes. Preheat the oven to 200°C and bake blind for 15 minutes. Remove the beans and paper, prick the pastry again, and return to the oven for 10 to 15 minutes until it is lightly browned. Whisk together the egg yolks, cream, mustard and seasoning. Stir in the Gruyère and feta. Remove the rind from the Brie, and cut it into ½ inch cubes, then stir it into the cream mixture. Whisk the egg whites until stiff and then fold them into the cream mixture. Pour into the pastry case and sprinkle a few pine nuts on top. Bake at 180°C for 35 minutes or until set. This tastes best if served at room temperature.

Apart from the company and the food my other clear memory from this party was that I used the river as an outdoor freezer for the wine and beer that we served. Clearing up after a dinner party of any size is always a chore and on this occasion I forgot about my improvised outdoor drinks fridge. Fortunately we didn't have much rain in the days following the party and the few unused cans of beer and bottles of wine were still resting among the pebbles in the river when I remembered them a week later. After more conventional dinner parties the leftovers usually consist of several portions of the different desserts that Ann likes to offer at such events. So I have the onerous task of eating them up in the days that follow. I like to think that this is a job I do particularly well.

16

Urban Myths

When we moved out of the city and into the Corvedale we had some idea of what country life would be like, because both of us had had experiences in our youth of visiting and staying in the country. Once we got here of course there was a lot more for us to learn. It didn't seem very difficult to pick up the social and cultural mores of the country. Two phrases sum up the approach that seemed to work for us; 'look and learn', and 'live and let live'. In my former life as a Probation Treatment Manager we called a similar skill 'perspective taking'. In other words, 'putting yourself in other people's shoes'. Once you adopt this approach it is relatively easy to work out why people behave in certain ways and to react accordingly.

Some of the differences we encountered were expected. Unlike most of our city friends who visited us in the first couple of years at the Mill, we were not astonished that when the sun went down it got dark. In 1984 it was really dark on a moonless night. When the moon was shining, and once you had accustomed your eyes to the dark, everything was lit by its beautiful, soft, pale light, in a way that I had never before experienced in the street-light lit city. Light pollution from Telford and Bridgnorth now intrudes a little on our night time skies, and more and more people are installing blazing 'security' lights, which I always think make their houses look like miniature open prisons, but clear moonlit nights are still one of my favourite aspects of living here.

We also quickly discovered that it is not quiet in the country, especially at night. Instead of the steady roar of traffic there is a basic silence that is regularly punctuated by sheep bleating, owls calling, cows lowing, and trees rustling in the wind. You also discover that lots of household appliances are quite noisy once it is quiet outside: fridges switch themselves on and off, clocks tick loudly, and the central heating pump starting up at 6.30 a.m. sounds like the next door neighbour trying to drill a hole in the wall. The distinction between outside and inside, so apparent in the city once you close your front door, is more nuanced in the country. It feels less like living in a small personal space surrounded by 'the outside', and more like being an integral part of the landscape, always interacting with it whether we are inside or outside the house.

Practical considerations shape many aspects of life in the Corvedale and often in ways that make the urban 'norm' irrelevant to country dwellers. Policies based on 'choice' often don't apply. There is only one primary school in the Corvedale and so there is no meaningful choice that parents of four year olds can exercise (unless of course they pay for private education). Ludlow now has only one Building Society branch so there is no choice there. Front page headlines about rises in gas prices pass us by since we don't have access to the gas network. More prosaically we have to think carefully about when and where we shop. Our nearest shop is 3 miles away, the nearest supermarket 9 miles distant. Even with the boon of freezers Ann has to plan what she is going to cook a week in advance, and it is partly as a result of this that we try hard not to waste any food. (Another factor here is the incredibly complicated procedure we are required to follow in order to dispose of any food waste, namely, wrap it in newspaper, store it in a brown box in the house and then once a fortnight carry it three hundred yards up to the council road and place it in a green wheely bin ready for collection by the Council.) Over the years a pattern has emerged whereby we eat certain meals on certain days. Whether by coincidence or not it is very traditional. We eat fish on Fridays because that is the day we do our weekly shop and so can buy fresh fish. On Sundays we have a roast dinner and the leftover meat is then used for at least one and often more meals through the rest of the week. On Mondays we always have curry, and always made to the same (traditional) recipe.

Mrs Finn's Curry

Cold roasted meat cut into pieces
¼ pint of day old gravy
½ tin tomatoes

1 teaspoon Fern's curry paste
1 small onion
Olive oil

Peel and chop the onion and fry it in a little olive oil until it is soft. Stir in the curry paste and turn up the heat. After 2 minutes add the gravy, tomatoes and cold meat. Simmer for about 15 to 20 minutes. Serve with basmati rice and natural yoghurt. Mrs

Finn was Ann's sister's mother in law and this is her genuine Indian recipe for making curry from the remains of a roasted joint of meat. Mrs Finn insisted that only Fern's curry paste (now quite hard to find) would do. We use the mild version.

The country landscape, beautiful though it is, is a workplace for most who live here. So just as we expected roads on industrial estates in Dudley to be mucky and congested with commercial vehicles, so we were not surprised to find that tractors drive slowly along our lanes, and that when they do they sometimes leave mud on the road. I remember making a joke to a neighbouring farmer soon after we moved here about having to clean my car every time I drove past his farm. He didn't smile, and at the time I thought that he was being unfriendly. Later I realised that like all farmers he has had encounters with people who have moved here from the city and who sincerely complain about mud on the roads and being held up by slow moving farm vehicles or, worse still, animals being driven down a lane. Years ago in Ludlow I was told about people who had bought a house next to a pub and then complained about the noise of people leaving it late at night. More recently, when the Ludlow church bells were removed for repair, a petition was started by people who had bought retirement apartments close to the church, asking that when they were re-installed they should no longer ring a peal to mark certain hours (as they had done for the previous five centuries or so) because they found the noise intrusive.

And then there are the people who have moved into Diddlebury, near to the dilapidated 1950s Village Hall, and who mounted a well organised, highly misleading, and ultimately successful campaign to prevent the Lottery supporting a scheme to build a new and bigger Hall. Their attitude appears to be that they have moved here to enjoy the peace and quiet of the countryside, not put up with lots of cars driving down the lane to and from a thriving community hall. Now they have arrived here they appear to want no further development to occur, presumably in case it 'spoils the village environment'. Some of them live in barn conversions which were working farm buildings when we came to the Corvedale. I think this is deeply ironic, but it does require some 'perspective taking' to see this.

The trail that we trod 27 years ago from the city to the countryside is now one that many people follow. Often they are retired (as we now are) and always they are, certainly in relation to us, well off. We paid £28,500 for our house in 1984 and it is now worth about £250,000. That 'profit' of £221,500 has been 'earned' by us through the simple and undemanding expedient of just living here. We have done nothing to deserve this windfall. The conditions necessary for us to enjoy this good fortune have been created by government through restrictions on the number of new houses built, selling off of council housing stock and inadequate provision of new social housing. There is therefore not enough housing to go round and so prices rise. The 'right' that many homeowners feel is theirs to make money simply by owning a property has been created deliberately by these means.

Rural poverty and rural homelessness are issues that have always concerned me since we moved here. In the 1990s I, along with others, set up a charity to advise and assist young homeless people in South Shropshire. It lasted for about 12 years or so before it ran out of funds and during that time helped hundreds of young people to find a home. As importantly, it influenced the local political agenda and helped to encourage innovative approaches to rural housing issues. The local housing association set up a 'foyer' for young people, borrowing a French model of independent living units with on site support workers and structured training programmes. The local council introduced an affordable housing policy that required all private developments over a certain size to have 50% of the units available for rent or shared equity ownership at prices that related to local wage levels. These were important policy initiatives, but the reality of 'the market' is that house prices in desirable areas like ours will always be inflated to levels that are out of reach for local people through the influx of people from other parts of the country, especially the South East of England, where house price inflation is highest. As this process continues, so the community that we have been privileged to be part of for the last 27 years will continue to atrophy until we reach the position, probably quite soon, where all the country areas are inhabited by retired incomers (plus the few remaining farmers) whose needs are serviced by workers housed in the market towns of the area. I don't want this to happen and will continue to do what I can to try to prevent it. We value the community in which we live very highly and don't want to lose it. Apart from that we want to carry on living here, and what is going to happen when the oil runs out?

17

Animals

The way in which most British people think about animals is often confused. We eat lots of meat but don't like to think about the fact that an animal has had to be killed in order to produce what we are eating. We certainly don't generally want to know anything about how that slaughtering actually occurs. Since living in the Corvedale we've tried to learn the 'country' way of thinking about these things but it has been hard to adjust. For example, at first we assumed that farmers would be very anxious if any of their stock escaped onto a road and so would be pleased and grateful if we telephoned them, even late at night, to tell them we'd seen a sheep or a cow that might be theirs. Unfortunately cattle and sheep escape from where they are supposed to be all the time and for many different reasons. If farmers dropped everything to chase after them every time this happened they would never get anything else done.

My first experience of this occurred many years ago before we even moved to the Corvedale. We had visited friends in mid Wales and were driving back in the late evening to Dudley through the Corvedale. Suddenly we came upon five or six sheep in the middle of the road. Having just about managed to avoid them through the combined effects of an emergency stop and a violent swerving manoeuvre I decided in my naïve public spirited way that 'someone' should be told about this situation. Just up the road was a pub called the *Seven Stars* and so I decided to call in there to see if anyone knew whose sheep might be in the middle of the B4368. I now know that the *Seven Stars* is a completely traditional, unspoilt, local pub that hasn't changed its approach, or probably its clientele, for 40 years. Back then it seemed like the pub in *American Werewolf in London* to me; I walked in, all conversation stopped, and all eyes seemed to turn on me. My opening line was, in retrospect, ill advised; "I haven't come in for a drink", I said, "there are some sheep in the road by the Holdgate turn". This prompted much puzzled muttering as people tried to understand why anyone would come into the Seven Stars if they didn't want a drink, and why this stranger was telling them about sheep being in the road. "I wondered if you knew whose sheep they might be", I suggested. The barman then asked various groups whose sheep they might be. A number of names were proposed, there was a lengthy discussion, and the name of Williams was agreed the most likely and conveyed back to me. (I now know, but didn't at the time, that there are umpteen farmers called Williams in the Corvedale.) The barman and I stood in silence, waiting for something more to occur. Eventually I said, "Perhaps you could ring him up to see if they are his sheep?" Clearly this possibility had not occurred to anyone up to that point and there was more animated conversation about what the number might be, and, more importantly, whether Mr Williams would welcome being telephoned late on a Saturday night to be told that a townie had recommended that he come and look at some sheep in the road to see if they belonged to him. I made my excuses and left.

More recently we experienced a variation on this scenario when we woke one morning and opened the curtains to find a flock of about 30 ewes munching their way through our and our neighbour's garden. We started telephoning the farmers closest to us but none of them had lost any sheep that fitted the description. Fortunately one of them must have recognised the 'tag' we'd described and made a further call because about half an hour later a farmer from Tugford arrived in his pick up and confirmed that they were his sheep, lost from a field over a mile away a couple of days before. I thought this was a sequence of events of great excitement and interest but his typically phlegmatic response was simply to say "I wondered where they'd got to", before getting his dog to drive them back up our lane and thence back home.

Knowledge of country living is still lacking among many urban dwellers but years ago it sometimes reached comical proportions. My step-daughter who is a teacher used to bring a couple of coach loads of her five and six year old pupils from Dudley for an 'exchange' visit with the Corvedale School every year. A local farmer used to give them a tour around the farm and answer their questions. Every year a common question would be, "Do you have television out here?". A highlight of the visit would be when the farmer brought in a large cardboard box, placed it in front of the assembled children and asked them to guess what was inside. From the box would come the unmistakable sounds of an angry cockerel but one year a little boy immediately raised his hand and being asked for his guess replied, "Please sir, it's a Hoover", thus demonstrating that he was better at reading than at animal recognition. These invaluable visits came to an end sometime in the nineties when it was deemed to be an unacceptable Health and Safety risk to show children around a farm.

Back in those days almost everyone that we knew kept a few chickens. Then Edwina Currie made her infamous remarks suggesting that Salmonella was present in almost all the chickens in the country, an hysterical food scare swept the pages of the daily newspapers, regulations were hurriedly brought in to appease the outcry, and almost everyone in the Corvedale who had been safely keeping chickens for eggs and meat for years gave them up as it was now too burdensome and expensive to comply with the new government requirements. For a long time we were unable to obtain free range chickens from anywhere except a specialist butchers shop in Ludlow, and then only at a price that made the meat a luxury. Thankfully

good flavoursome free range chickens are now more readily available and it's often a safe bet for the main course of a dinner party. That doesn't mean that it has to be boring. Ann has used her knowledge and experience of Greek cuisine to produce this fabulously rich and tasty chicken dish which always goes down well (in every sense of the phrase) when we have friends round for dinner.

Greek Style Roast Chicken

A medium/large (about 4lb) free range chicken
1 lemon
3 floz olive oil
½ tablespoon sea salt
1 lb Potatoes, peeled and cut into quarters

3 cloves of unpeeled garlic
3 tablespoons of dried oregano
3 bay leaves
10 floz chicken stock
1 tablespoon wholegrain mustard
Butter
Pepper

Preheat the oven to 190°C. Put the chicken in a roasting dish and rub the olive oil over it. Do the same with the juice from the lemon and then sprinkle some salt over the bird. Arrange the potatoes and garlic all around the chicken. Sprinkle some more olive oil over the potatoes. Smear the mustard on top of the chicken and then sprinkle oregano and pepper over it. Arrange the bay leaves among the potatoes. Now pour half the chicken stock over the potatoes only and put a big knob of butter on top of the chicken. Roast in the oven uncovered for 15 minutes and then turn the oven down to 180°C. Roast for a further 90 minutes, basting the chicken and potatoes every 20 minutes or so. If the liquid dries up add some more stock to the potatoes. On removal from the oven the chicken should be browned on top and the potatoes will be soft and rich, having absorbed all the juices from the cooking. Ann usually uses Maris Piper potatoes if she can get them. Her stock of dried oregano was bought in Sivota in the Epiros region of Greece some years ago from a man selling bags of wild dried oregano from under the plane tree in the village square.

We have never kept chickens, and apart from the first few years at the Mill we've never had a dog, but we have always had a cat. Our present cat Rosie (age 17) is pictured on p113 top right. Cats can be very useful for rodent control when mice, rats and squirrels try to share your country idyll. Our best ratter was a male cat called Basil (pictured on p113, top left). He seemed to be fearless and would bring back dead prey in triumph and carefully place them on the doorstep so we could see how good a hunter

he was. On one occasion he brought back a dead stoat, on another a dead cock pheasant. When our French friends Peter and Christine were visiting us at Broncroft for the first time Basil must have felt a bit neglected. We had just got home from a trip to Shrewsbury. Basil meowed outside the door and without looking through the window I automatically let him in. In ran Basil with a large live rat in his mouth, which he then dropped on the floor. The rat ran behind the dresser and Basil then showed no further interest in it and started washing himself. I think he was probably attention seeking. If so he must have been delighted with the reaction that he elicited from us. Shouting at Peter and Christine to stay upstairs and close all the doors we then spent the next half an hour carefully moving everything in the hallway that a rat could hide behind until eventually it ran out and escaped back into the outside world.

18

Weather

Like many older people we've been amused by the way in which today's 24-hour rolling news media reported the weather over the last two unusually cold winters. In Shropshire we escaped the worst of the snow but we had quite a bit, so our schools were closed just like everyone else's. Not only that, our recycling collections were suspended for five weeks, yes five weeks, because the back lanes were a bit icy. We wondered how they would have coped in 1985 and 1986. In the first three years after we moved to the Mill in 1984 we had what then we regarded as severe winters and what now would be reported as more or less the end of the world. During one of them Sandy Lane near us had several inches of solid ice covering it for at least a week. As far as I remember I managed to negotiate this in my car and get to work in Dudley, thirty two miles away, without too much difficulty. Another year the same lane was filled with snow to a depth of about seven feet. That did snow me in for a day or two and a snow blower had to be summoned to clear it as it was too deep for a snow plough to deal with. In these conditions we quickly learnt a number of important lessons. The first was about wood for the fire. We had assumed that it would be simple to buy wood in the country but this isn't always the case. In addition, wood needs to be seasoned for at least two years before it is ready to burn in anything like an efficient way. So when we ran out of wood during our first winter we were in some trouble. Our friend Roy from Knighton came to our rescue by arranging for his friend

Brian to deliver some wood to us. Brian arrived in a car, towing a trailer, and proceeded to unload the greenest, sappiest load of oak I have ever seen. Then he couldn't get his car back up our drive because of the snow, so we had to summon help from our (at this stage new) neighbours. They rather reluctantly helped us to push Brian's car back up to the lane, during which procedure Brian became quite agitated and began to loudly bemoan the fact that if we didn't hurry up he would be late for his date to have tea and cakes with Princess Anne in Bridgnorth. I don't know what drugs he was on at the time but they were obviously quite strong.

So we learned that we need to keep a good stock of wood so that we don't run short. The motto is 'you can never have too much wood'. In the last few years we have had the money to install two Clearview log burners and these make the house warm and snug in even the coldest conditions (minus 19°C on one night in December 2010). Fortunately we can still buy wood from local suppliers and we now have a policy of buying wood well in advance so that the wood we have bought this winter will be used at the earliest in two years time. Cold weather also has an influence on what we eat. We keep a good stock of frozen pre-prepared meals in case we are snowed in, and a stock of tinned food in case we are snowed in and the power goes down. When it is just cold we eat food that is cheery and warming. I've always found that curries are good in these circumstances, as well as being an excellent way to use up meat leftovers and thus put off for another day the need to drive to the shops on icy roads. If we want a change from *Mrs Finn's Curry* (see p105) and we are stuck at home 'for the duration' Ann often cooks this robust alternative, which is started on one day and finished and eaten on the following day.

Beef And Beer Curry

1½lb stewing beef, cut into cubes
4oz chopped onions
1½ teaspoons of Fern's curry paste
1lb peeled and chopped tomatoes
2 tablespoons olive oil

For the marinade:
½ teaspoon salt
1 teaspoon black pepper

1 teaspoon ground cinnamon
1 teaspoon ground cumin
1 teaspoon dry mustard
2 garlic cloves, crushed
½ teaspoon Cayenne pepper
1 teaspoon allspice
4oz onions, finely chopped
½ pint brown ale or stout

Preheat the oven to 200°C. Prepare the marinade by mixing the dry spices and the chopped onions, and then adding the meat cubes and the beer. Mix together, cover, and put on one side overnight. When you are ready to cook the curry, fry the onions in the olive oil. Add the curry paste and fry the mixture for a few minutes and then add the tomatoes and continue stirring over a very low heat for a further 10 minutes. Remove from the heat and stir in the meat and marinade. Put the mixture in a covered casserole dish in the oven and cook for an hour. If the meat is not quite tender after this time cook for another 30 minutes, adding a little water if the liquid has evaporated. Serve with rice.

Everyone in the UK has become more accustomed to extreme weather in the last few years as heavy downpours of rain, in particular, have become more common and widespread. For 23 years we lived beside the Tug Brook without ever worrying about the possibility of flooding, but in the summer of 2007 we had two near misses during periods of intense slow moving rain bands which brought flooding to several other parts of the country at the same time. Tug Brook is actually several yards wide as it passes our house and when it is in flood it can be over 6 feet deep. We had several anxious hours watching the level rise up to the bottom of the wooden Council footbridge that forms part of a public footpath before it receded again. On one of these two days we had our only sighting of an otter in Shropshire. Ann saw it first and shouted to me to look. Sure enough, stationary in the raging torrent, an otter stared at me as I stared at it. I presume that it took so much energy for the creature to hold its position against the flow while it drew breath that it had none left over to take evasive action when it saw me. After about 20 seconds it disappeared below the surface. We think that it had probably swum upstream from the River Corve in order to get away from the flood, keeping as deep as possible where the current would be less violent, but having to come up to the surface for air from time to time. It was our good fortune that it chose our stretch of river for an air break and that we happened to be there at that moment to witness it.

It was also our good fortune in 2007 that we were not flooded. In September 2008 we had another similar 'weather event' but this time we came off worse. After an afternoon of again watching the level of the river rise up to the bottom of the footbridge, there was then an additional surge of water that raised the level by another foot or so. Subsequently we discovered that there had been a terrific cloudburst across the slopes of Brown Clee hill such that car drivers had to stop in the road because they literally could not see anything ahead through the rain. When the run off reached our house it was blocked by the footbridge and so came out and around our house. It took very little time for it to get to a depth of a couple of feet; and indeed I only just had enough time to get sandbags from the shed (obtained from the Council after the 2007 floods) and put them against the door. Notwithstanding these, the pressure of the water was so great that Ann, who was inside the house, had to use towels and blankets to try to confine the incoming water to the hallway. Meanwhile I was outside with my friend Wyndham, who had nobly answered Ann's frantic phone call asking for help, and we were trying to knock a hole in the stone wall and iron railings that separates our garden from the river so that the water could drain back into it. The noise from the torrent was so great that we had to shout in each other's ears to be heard. I remember feeling quite anxious and very intimidated by the relentless and seemingly unstoppable surge of foaming brown water, but even in these circumstances I could not help but smile to myself when Wyn's wife Bronwen warned him to be careful that he did not fall into the water as he was not a good swimmer. Anyone falling into that torrent would have been dashed against a tree or rock within a few seconds. Just as I was inwardly resigning myself to a year of insurance claims and flood damage repairs I saw the footbridge start to bend under the force of the water pressing against it. Shouting at Wyn to watch out we stepped back from the brink just as the bridge came adrift from its supports and hurtled past us, demolishing a young bankside oak tree as it did so, and then disappeared downstream. The level of water around the house immediately began to subside and within 15 minutes it had gone, leaving behind a covering of silt over everything. This is my picture of Wyndham knocking down the wall, with Bronwen standing on the lawn, as the flood water began to recede.

The best remembered days of course are those when the sun shone from a clear blue sky and the only sounds were the birds singing and the brook babbling. It was a day like that when we moved to Broncroft Mill. The way the human mind works is fascinating to me, and one aspect is the way we associate different things together because they once occurred together on a memorable occasion. We were subconsciously convinced that the sun always shone at Broncroft simply because this is what it did on the day we moved there. Similarly, I have to stop myself thinking of Sheffield, a city I have great affection for, as always being cold and wet and a little bit grey and depressing. We always visit our friends there in the winter (generally February), for the entirely sensible reason that we like to do 'city things' (cinema, theatre, shopping etc) when we go there and these can all be done in any weather. So all my memories of Sheffield are locked in the context of dark afternoons and rainy or icy pavements and streets. When our Sheffield friends visit us they come in the summer so that we can enjoy country walks and aperitifs on the lawn before dinner. Ann likes to try out food for warm days on these occasions and a particular favourite is this one.

Coronation Chicken

3½lb chicken portions
1 small onion
Olive oil
1 teaspoon Ferns curry paste
¼ pint red wine
½ pint chicken stock
½ teaspoon tomato purèe

The juice of ½ a lemon
1 bay leaf
2 tablespoons apricot jam or chutney
½ pint mayonnaise (or ¼ pint thick
   yoghurt mixed with ¼ pint mayonnaise)
Chopped pineapple

Poach the chicken gently in the red wine and chicken stock. When cooked, cut into bite size portions. Peel and chop the onion and fry in the oil. Stir in the curry paste. Add the wine, tomato puree, lemon juice, a little water, the apricot jam or chutney, and the bay leaf and simmer for about 15 minutes until syrupy. Allow it to cool and then stir in the chicken and mayonnaise. This can be served with rice made with equal quantities of rice and vegetables. If desired you can pour on a French dressing an hour before serving.

So far we have managed to cope with all the different types of weather that the Corvedale has thrown at us. While there have certainly been some moments and periods of concern and anxiety the only time that the weather has truly frightened me occurred in London in 1987 when I found myself caught up in the 'Great Hurricane'. I had gone with a friend to South East London to do some training for a private training company and we were staying with the owner and his wife in their flat. The wind started to pick up soon after we arrived there and by the evening was quite strong. I remember our host and his wife had an argument because she wanted him to move his car from the road to their driveway and he couldn't be bothered to go out in the wind and rain to do this. We drank some beer and went to bed at about midnight. My friend and I were in sleeping bags on the floor of the attic room, which was in the roof space of the three-storey house. We went to sleep at first but were woken in the early hours by the howling of the wind and a strange cacophony of sound made up of smashing roof slates and tiles, dustbins crashing into walls, branches of trees being ripped off and dogs barking from all corners of the city. The really scary time was when I could feel the joists moving under my head as I lay on the floor trying to sleep.

In the morning we heard on the radio that a hurricane had struck, and we noted that a tree had fallen across our host's driveway at just the point where he should have left his car had he not been so lazy the night before. Unsurprisingly the power was also off and our host seemed to be completely devastated by this and spent 20 minutes frantically ringing friends and relations to see if their power was also off. We struggled to understand what the point of this was and perhaps on that day we had a brief insight into the chaos that may occur in the cities when our energy supplies become more expensive and less reliable in the future. We are accustomed to the power going off during and after storms and keep torches, candles, bottled gas stoves etc ready for such an eventuality. With a log burner and food from the store cupboard we can get by for a week without electricity if necessary. City life is perhaps so utterly dependent on electricity that people may genuinely be unable to cope if it ever goes off for any length of time.

We abandoned our training course and headed back to the Midlands along roads turned bright green with the thousands of leaves the storm had scattered, and through woods laid completely flat by the storm.

19

Student Days

I was an undergraduate student for three years at Leicester University and a postgraduate student for two years at Cardiff University. Of the two cities I preferred Cardiff by far. It was small enough to get to know and to get around with ease and yet because it is a capital city it had far more going on than other UK cities of its size (Leicester for example). There was plenty of theatre, music, cinema, art etc on offer and I was a regular consumer of all of these. In addition there were open spaces, and nearby countryside, and great pubs serving good beer. The puerile thrill of going up to the bar and asking for "a pint of Brain's" took a while to wear off but I've never lost my taste for a pint of 'S.A.'; presumably meant to be short for 'Special Ale' but always known in Cardiff as 'Skull Attack'.

In the circle of friends that I moved in when I was in Cardiff, almost all of whom were, like me, social work students, there was a group of us who would regularly go out to pubs where traditional jazz was played. In the seventies, when I was there, this was a thriving scene, and although trad jazz is not one of my most favourite musical genres, when it is played with enthusiasm in crowded (and as they were then, smoky) bars it's a great evening's entertainment. There were a number of pubs with regular trad jazz nights; one I remember was next to the railway station. After a while we got to know some of the bands and occasionally we would go to a new pub to see one of our favourites. One of these was a trumpet player whose name I cannot now remember but who was a musical cut above most of the other musicians in this scene. He and his newly formed quartet were playing in a pub we had not visited before and a small group of us decided to attend. As we followed, on foot, the directions we had been given, we realised, with some apprehension, that the venue was in docklands. In Cardiff at that time the railway line divided the cosmopolitan city from the notorious backstreets of Tiger Bay. As well brought up middle class students, going 'the other side of the tracks' at night, on foot, was just a little bit scary. So with some trepidation we sought out the pub, a tiny, typical, basic, back street local, bought a drink, and crammed ourselves around one of the scrubbed tables. The trumpet player recognised us and was pleased to see us. He and his band played well and the evening passed off without incident. One of our friends even struck up a conversation during the break with a couple of the locals. The next day he told us that the topic of the conversation had been the incident a few days before that had taken place around the table where we had sat. Apparently two men had sat there arguing and drinking for a long time until their anger and drunkenness had reached a crescendo, and one of the men had staggered out and left. The other man remained and seemed to have slumped into a drunken stupor. In pubs like this people kept themselves to themselves and so it was a good half an hour before someone had had the nerve to approach the man to ask if he was alright, only for him to slump forward and reveal a knife stuck in his innards. We never really found out whether this story was true or apocryphal but it certainly seemed sufficiently plausible for us never to go there again!

When I was a student I had very little money and spent as little of it as possible on food. I can hardly believe it now but I used to survive for weeks at a time on a diet of cheese and potato pie, marmite sandwiches and omelettes. I'm ashamed to say that my budgets for cigarettes and beer seemed much more important to me in those days. Admittedly we did drink Lapsang Souchong and Orange Pekoe tea and eat scones and jam during the Test Match tea interval as we lounged on the lawn listening to the cricket commentary on a transistor radio during my second summer at Leicester, but that was very much an exception to the rule. I certainly never bought cake, but occasionally I would indulge myself and make my 'fridge' cake. It became a favourite with my housemates and so after a while we shared the cost and always kept a supply on hand for celebratory or commiseratory occasions.

Hollywood Cake

4oz margarine
4oz sugar
4oz dried fruit
1 egg

8oz digestive biscuits
1 tablespoon cocoa
8oz cooking chocolate

Melt the sugar and margarine in a pan. Add the beaten egg, cocoa, dried fruit and crushed biscuits. Spread this mixture on a greased tray and place in the fridge until it is set. Melt the chocolate in a bowl over a pan of hot water. Spread this over the set mixture and put back in the fridge until this is set. Cut into small square portions.

I didn't enjoy Leicester as much as Cardiff, partly because I took a while to find settled living and social circumstances. In my final year though I ended up in self-catering university accommodation and fell in with some like-minded people. Our sense of humour was rather childish and somewhat esoteric. It also got us into a lot of trouble when we decided to have a party. Not content with inviting all our friends we decided we ought to find some event which we could pretend we were commemorating. A search through the reference books revealed that the date we had set was that on which General Redvers-Buller relieved the siege of the town of Mafeking during the Boer War. This was obscure enough to appeal to our sense of the absurd and so we made a large banner, inscribed the words 'Welcome to General Redvers-Buller' on it, and strung it across the outside of the house. 'What a laugh' we thought. Other people thought 'we have no idea what those weirdoes are trying to convey but they must be having a party tonight so we'll go along'. By 9pm there was a seething mass of several hundred people outside the house, and inside another hundred were crammed together like sardines. It was a 'Facebook gatecrash' 1970s style. For reasons that I no longer recall I was nominated to exit the house by the back door, run right around the outside of the site to the front entrance and use the public telephone there to call the police. This I did, and after bizarrely getting the engaged tone when I first dialled 999, I eventually managed to request police back up. Ten minutes later a very bored police sergeant turned up in a van, listened to my rather hysterical explanation of the situation, and then patiently pushed his way through the crowd until he got to the front door. Here he turned around to face the mob and told them in a loud voice to go home because the party was full. Astoundingly this is exactly what most of them did.

We had another encounter with the emergency services during that year only this time it was the fire brigade. Next door to our house was a large Victorian property which had been converted into an old people's home. One day a discarded cigarette or a reckless or malicious teenager set the shrubbery between the two properties on fire. Flames were leaping high in the air and residents of the home were cowering on the fire escape stairs in some distress. With what we thought was an exemplary display of public spiritedness several of us grabbed the fire extinguishers from the house, rushed out, and discharged them onto the seat of the flames. To everyone's relief we succeeded in reducing the fire to a smouldering mass of burnt vegetation, at which point a fire engine arrived, all lights flashing and all sirens sounding. Out piled the fire-fighters only to find a group of hairy students prancing around with fire extinguishers. We thought they would be pleased we had done their job for them but we could not have been more wrong. In very disgruntled fashion they tried to order us outside into the road, which we refused to do since we were in the grounds of our own house. They then stomped through the remains of the fire doing very exaggerated 'damping down' procedures while the section leader radioed 'fire out' back to base in a disappointed tone. All the while we were prancing

around taking wacky photos and basking in the acclaim of the large group of fellow students who had by this time gathered to watch the fun.

We regarded ourselves as heroes but the university authorities didn't share this view. When we applied to have our fire extinguishers replaced/ refilled we were told we would have to pay for this as we hadn't used them to fight a fire on university property. Our neighbours in the old people's home were more sympathetic and gave us tea and cakes as a thank you.

20

Football

've had a strange relationship with football over the years. As a youngster I was as keen as all my mates to kick a ball around on the 'rec' (i.e. the recreation ground). Perhaps because of a combination of my height and my cautious temperament I found that centre half was my best position. Obviously I'm talking about the sixties when we had positions like centre half and inside left, and the numbers on the shirts told you which position the player played in rather than who they were. Sadly I have never in my life worn the 'number 5 shirt' of a centre half in a proper game of football because the school that I attended refused to allow such a common sport and insisted that everyone should play 'rugger' in the winter.

My first experience of rugby was as an eleven year old. We had some sort of say in which position we played and as all I knew about rugby was that the full back took the kicks and since I enjoyed kicking a ball I volunteered for that position. Nobody told me that the full back is also the last line of defence. Our first serious game was against another team who were bigger and stronger than us and so on more than one occasion I was faced with a line of large boys bearing down on me. Just as they got to me they would pass the ball and thus evade my attempts to get it but would also make sure they flattened me in the process. From this experience I developed the view that rugby is really about the physical confrontation and that the ball is a secondary factor. I also acquired my life long loathing for the game, which was reinforced in my student days by the drunken and delinquent 'high jinks' that the rugby players would indulge in at the student bars every Saturday evening.

Playing football every break time on the school parade ground (you see what a posh school it was) was no substitute for playing on a proper pitch. I used to be quite a good defender but I'll never know how I would have performed in a proper game. Of course you don't need to play football to be a football supporter and like most boys I was keen to bestow my allegiance on a team. As a Brummie I was surrounded by mates who all supported either Villa or the Blues. Unfortunately by this time I had already been poached by a different team, little knowing that once you become a football supporter you are saddled with your team for life.

As an only child I looked forward to school holidays with great excitement because my two male cousins from Lancashire would always come to visit for a week. The oldest of the two is about 7 years older than me so that when I was about eight he was fifteen or sixteen, and in my eyes a 'grown up'. At this impressionable age he was my hero and could do no wrong and there was no question but that I should become a fan of his team, Manchester City. This was the sixties when City were pretty good and their United rivals were often second best. Of course since then I have learnt that City fans have to be stoical at all times and I've had to put up with the jibes of my other cousin, Nigel, nearer my age and who later on I bonded with almost as a brother, who of course supports United. Maybe by the time you read this the tables might have been turned again?

During my teenage years I visited Lancashire to stay with my cousins more often than anywhere else and I acquired a great affection for the county and its people. The only other part of the country I visited regularly in those days was London, where my mother's family all were, and I was always struck by how much more friendly the average Lancashire person in the street was than his or her counterpart in the south east. When I visited Chorley me and my cousin Nigel played golf together, listened to Jimi Hendrix and John Mayall records together and generally shared every interest except the football team we supported. When I got a car in my early twenties my first long distance drive was a trip up the M6 to Lancashire, and I continued to visit in the following years. When I wrote to confirm the details of the visit (no email or mobile phones in those days) I would generally add a postscript asking if Nigel's wife Vicky would make me a favourite dessert while I was there. Even after my visits to Lancashire became more infrequent I never forgot how good Vicky's Pavlova Cake tasted and many years later she was kind enough to give the recipe to Ann.

Pavlova Cake

For the meringue:
3 egg whites
6oz caster sugar
1 teaspoon corn flour
¼ teaspoon vanilla essence
1 teaspoon lemon juice

For the filling:
½ pint whipping cream
4oz raspberries
4oz cherries
4 apricots
2 peaches

Draw a seven inch circle on parchment paper and place in a baking tray. Whisk the egg whites until stiff and dry. Sieve and whisk in half of the sugar and continue whisking until the mixture is stiff and shiny. Sieve the remaining sugar with the corn flour and fold into the mixture with the lemon juice and vanilla essence. Spread the meringue on the circle and build up into a bowl shaped shell. Bake in the centre of a slow oven for 1¼ to 1½ hours until it is firm and delicately coloured. Allow to cool before removing the parchment. The shell can be stored in an airtight container until required. For the filling simply whip the cream and place it in the meringue shell and then arrange the fruit in it as you wish.

It was of course unthinkable that Nigel, a Man Utd fan, would take me to Maine Road to see City, and in any case I usually visited in the summer during football's close season. So although I've watched City at Bolton, Wolves, West Brom and Leicester I've never seen them at home, and indeed I've never seen them win. It was frustrating living so far away from Maine Road and in any case I had no-one to go to matches with. So in my late teens I began to support a 'second' team, Wolves. My mate Alf was Tipton born and bred and every so often he would take me to matches. We always stood on the North Bank with the home supporters and the repartee from the crowd was usually as riveting as the action on the pitch, sometimes more so. This was the era of Phil 'Elvis' Parkes in goal and Steve 'Tank' Kindon on the wing. I asked Alf how they got their nicknames. "Watch Parkes when he collects the ball", he said, and sure enough, the goalkeeper would preen his hair and look behind him to the packed North Bank for applause every time he caught the ball. Kindon's moniker was easier to understand since his one and only mode of playing seemed to be to get the ball and then run at full pelt with it towards the opposition goal until either he ran it out into touch, or he was dispossessed or, occasionally, he scored. He must have been an only child too, with only imaginary team-mates to pass to. This was also the era of the sublime Peter Knowles who curtailed his career when he was poised to achieve greatness, I think to join an evangelical cult. He was a joy to watch: I haven't seen many players 'live' but he and Colin Bell are the two that I did see play who really did make you believe you were watching 'the beautiful game'.

21

Scotland

I f you watch the BBC weather forecast you would think that Scotland is the size of a few English counties. It's only when you get there that you realise that it really is a different and surprisingly large country. Watching the BBC news in Scotland, at least since devolution, confirms this for the visitor, as does the receipt of unfamiliar looking banknotes in your change. Ann always tries to spend these before we return to England as though they were the equivalent of Euros or Dollars. In recent years our trips north have been to Mallaig, in the north west Highlands, to stay in a holiday bungalow owned, and occasionally let out, by friends. It's a journey of well over 400 miles from Broncroft and although we have on one occasion completed it in one go we generally stop over in the Borders and take two days for the journey. The first time we went I thought that once we crossed the border into Scotland we were almost there. In fact we had not even got to the half way point. Scotland is a big country, and when you are in the Highlands the Scottish government in Edinburgh can doubtless seem as remote as London often seems for us in the Welsh Marches. The scenery of course is as spectacular as the weather is unpredictable.

In the 1990s Ann's sister and her husband moved to Arbroath on the north east coast of Scotland and so we visited there on a number of occasions. The local people seemed less friendly than in other parts of Scotland and I was not surprised to learn that the Scottish National Party (SNP) is strong in that region. On the other hand the frosty reception I sometimes seemed to receive from Scots on visits to Mick and Joan might have been for other reasons. As a golfer I was, of course, always keen to play in Scotland and my brother in law Mick would kindly arrange games for me with golfing colleagues from the F.E. College where he had gone to take up a Vice Principal position. These fellow golfers would always be courteous but also rather distant, as though we were playing a County match rather than just a friendly round of golf. Then after one game I was told by my host that he had enjoyed our game having not expected to do so. Another round of drinks and some further enquiries revealed that Mick, who as an Englishman had clearly been on the receiving end of some nationalistic 'stick' from his Scottish subordinates at the college, had arranged my 'friendly' games with his golfing colleagues on the basis that I was a fiercely competitive and proudly nationalistic English golfer who would doubtless give them a good thrashing on the course and show them how the game should really be played. No wonder my welcome from my hosts, affronted by the idea of entertaining a boastful Sassenach at their club but nervous of offending their boss by refusing to do so, was so guarded! I should say that all these games ended up in good friendly spirit and I was privileged to get to play wonderful courses like Edzell and Carnoustie.

One of the ways in which I broke the ice with my frosty Scottish golfing partners was by raising the topic of Scotch malt whisky. I first developed a liking for single malts when Glenfiddich was about the only single malt that was generally available south of the border. Now of course there are hundreds and hundreds of different 'expressions' as they are called, readily available from dozens and dozens of different distilleries. I don't drink whisky often and so a bottle will last me for several years, especially now that I have about 20 different bottles to choose from. Whenever I'm in Scotland I try to visit a distillery and buy a bottle there (Bladnoch was the most recent) or go to a specialist whisky shop and make a purchase. Spending £40 or £50 on one bottle of whisky somehow seems acceptable when I'm on holiday and using a credit card. When we visited Edinburgh for the first time in 1998 I was very keen to go into the Cadenhead's whisky shop on the Royal Mile and once inside I was not disappointed. After about ten minutes of browsing I plucked up courage to ask, as an Englishman, for a whisky I could not see displayed on their shelves.

In the early 90s, just as malts began to be more widely available, I had bought a bottle of Longrow 1974 16 year old malt whisky from an Oddbins

shop in Shrewsbury. The only reason I bought it was that it was in their sale, marked down to £20. I remember that the bottle was perched on the top of their shelves, had to be retrieved by use of a set of steps, and was covered in dust. It was the finest malt I have ever tasted and after it was all gone I tried to buy another bottle. None of the Shropshire off licences I went in had even heard of it and so whenever we were visiting other parts of the country Ann would urge me to go into off licences and enquire. Always I received only a blank stare and by the time we arrived in Cadenhead's on the Royal Mile I had become fed up with asking. So it was only because of Ann's prompting that I again made my weary request. This time I did get an answer, which was "we haven't got any Longrow in stock but we can put you on our list if you like". A conversation developed and I learned that Longrow was only made during a brief period each year (at the Campbeltown distillery that makes Springback for the rest of the year) and that in the next few weeks the shop would receive their limited allocation of bottles. Would I like to put my name down for a bottle? I think the price was £42, a lot of money for me to find then, and so it was only after some hesitation that I agreed, and handed over my credit card. While we were completing the transaction process I asked what type of Longrow it would be. They bottle at ten years old now I was told. "So it won't be 1974 16 year old then", I asked, "only I had a bottle of that once and it was absolutely delicious". The shopkeeper replied that this particular version of Longrow was indeed recognised by the cognoscenti to be a very fine malt but it was now almost impossible to find. Only the month before he had been at a whisky auction and a bottle had sold for £1250. We left the shop in a state of shock and continued our sightseeing tour of the city which was punctuated every half hour or so for the rest of the day by Ann suddenly turning to me and saying in a tone of incredulous rebuke "£1250!!!.......and you drank it!!!"

All the whisky books, of which there are now many, suggest that some malts go very well with a slice of fruit cake.

Scottish Fruit Cake

8oz self raising flour
4oz soft brown sugar
2oz glacé cherries
4floz oil
½ teaspoon almond extract
A pinch of salt

½ teaspoon mixed spice
10–12oz mixed fruit
2 eggs
4floz milk
1oz demerara sugar

Sift the flour, salt and spice into a bowl. Add the rest of the ingredients except the Demerara sugar. Beat until everything is mixed together well. Turn the mixture into a 7 inch square or 8 inch round tin. Sprinkle with Demerara sugar and bake for 2 hours at 150°C.

Thinking about Scotland always makes me think of my friend Alistair, who was a colleague of mine in Dudley in the eighties. Alistair and his wife Margaret have lived in Spain for the last several years and when we visited them a few years ago they made us very welcome. They took us to some authentic Spanish restaurants where we especially enjoyed the paella but they also cooked some delicious food for us at their home. We particularly enjoyed this recipe of Alistair's for spare ribs.

Alistair's Spare Ribs

4lb pork spare ribs or chops
2 tablespoons oil
Salt

For the sauce:
1 large onion finely chopped
1 garlic clove crushed with ½ teaspoon
  of salt
1 tablespoon tomato purée

2 tablespoons soy sauce
1 tablespoon soft brown sugar
1 tablespoon clear honey
Pepper
½ pint chicken stock
The juice of ½ lemon
4oz mixed dried fruit (prunes, apricots
  and apples soaked overnight and
  drained)

Sprinkle the pork with salt and place in a roasting tin. Pour the oil over it and roast in the oven at 190°C for 30 minutes. Remove from the oven and cut into bite size pieces. Now prepare the sauce by heating a spoonful of oil in a small pan. Add the onion and garlic and fry gently for 5 minutes or until golden. Remove from the heat and stir in the remaining sauce ingredients, adding pepper to taste. Mix well. Now return the meat to the roasting tin and pour the sauce over it. Cover the tin and continue roasting for a further 90 minutes or until the meat is tender. About 20 minutes before the end of the cooking time remove the tin from the oven, add the mixed dried fruit, and return to the oven for the final 20 minutes roasting. Serve with rice.

Alistair comes from Dunfermline, which he would always say is in the Kingdom of Fife. We went up there a couple of times on short golfing holidays and I loved the area. On the way up Alistair would instruct me on which Scottish football teams played in which towns. For example, "where do Raith Rovers play?" (Answer: Kirkcaldy). "What about Queen of the South?" (Answer: Dumfries). In Fife we would meet up with Alistair's nephew, who was only a few years younger than him, and was known as 'wee Archie'. Wee Archie was a biker who had served in the Black Watch as the Colonel's batman and was as far as I was concerned the salt of the earth. On our first visit he took us to his local pub in Crossgates (pronounced 'Crozzgates') on the night that England were playing Scotland at Wembley live on the pub telly. When I opened my mouth the pub went silent. If I had not been with Archie I doubt I would have got out alive. Our second visit the next year coincided with my birthday and Archie gave me a Scottish pound note (still then legal tender) which is still in my wallet as a reminder of a great character, who tragically died suddenly of a heart attack a few years ago.

22

Pat

Read any autobiography and you will find the author confidently outlining the thoughts and feelings they experienced during their childhood. I suppose that most of us take it for granted that their memories are accurate. But when I come to think about my childhood I struggle to remember even the most basic events, let alone what I was feeling on my first date, or when I opened the envelope containing my O-level results. I can make a good guess at how I felt when those things happened, but that is what it would be – a guess, not an actual memory. Perhaps this is how auto biographers proceed. Perhaps my childhood was unusually secure and uneventful. I do remember that by the time I was doing A-levels, aged 17, I was desperate to leave home and escape from what to me seemed the boring security of loving parents of an only child. And I also remember the fear in the pit of my stomach at the prospect of fending for myself in 'the big wide world'.

So I arranged a 'gap' year working for Community Service Volunteers (CSV). They assigned me to work as an unqualified teacher in a Children's Home (as they were then called) in Wandsworth, South London. In those days children who were taken into the care of the local authority in Wandsworth were placed in Earlsfield House while they were assessed and a long term plan for their care agreed. During this time they continued their education at local primary or secondary schools, as long as these would accept them. Many of the children had 'special needs' and so could not be placed in an outside school. These would all be taught in the tuition unit within the institution. My task was to assist the head teacher of the unit in her classroom. Her name was Pat.

All the children in the tuition unit were, by definition, unable to cope with ordinary schooling. They were all troubled; quite a few were troublesome. Some came with labels such as 'maladjusted' or 'educationally subnormal' or 'autistic'. Others had not been assigned to a category or given a diagnosis to explain their 'abnormal' behaviour. Some had been subjected to dreadful sexual and/or physical abuse by parents or relatives. Others seemed to be simply the victims of unhappy circumstances. Pat treated each and every child as an individual with needs to be met and potential to be fulfilled. She would not allow any physical chastisement in the unit (very much against the norm for the times) and would go to extraordinary lengths to try to meet the educational and developmental needs of her pupils. I remember one girl, aged about 6 or 7, who was autistic. She would not or could not use words, but would communicate in grunts and squeals or, often, screams. She was clearly intelligent and would play with paint and toys in a very creative way. If she was calm she would listen with great concentration, and apparent understanding, to a story being read aloud. This was one of my jobs. After about a month in the unit she had become markedly less troubled in her behaviour and demeanour. Then she was returned to her mother, no school would take her, and she regressed. Pat somehow arranged for her to be allowed to continue attending the unit, but sometimes her mother would not be able or willing to get her to the unit on the bus. When this happened Pat would drive with me to the girl's home in her old Vauxhall with a bench front seat, steering wheel gear shift and no seatbelts, and we would then collect the girl and take her to school. If she was in an aggressive, unco-operative mood, which was often, I would have to sit her on my lap in the front passenger seat and try to restrain her from hitting or biting me, or Pat, or the gear shift as we drove through the south London morning rush hour. No doubt today this would contravene no end of guidelines and regulations. But Pat could see that this girl needed the support and stimulation that we could give her in the unit and she was not going to allow mere practicalities to get in the way of meeting those needs.

Outside her job Pat was unceasingly active in her local Labour Party, with local mental health charities, CND, and many other progressive causes. She had a wide circle of friends, of all ages, and was interested in theatre, books, and all things cultural. She was warm and funny, treated me like an adult and encouraged me to take responsibility and think for myself.

Pat held regular dinner parties and I would sometimes be invited. I would be spellbound as the conversation rolled around the table, flowing and building and twisting like a river in flood as each person (except me) added some interesting opinion or remark, or challenged a political view, or introduced a completely new but linked topic or argument. I don't remember much about what we ate at these events, except for this distinctive dessert, which has since become a firm favourite in our household. I can clearly remember Pat placing what looked to me like a lump of suet in the middle of the table and then cutting it open to reveal the lemon wallowing in the delicious juices inside.

Sussex Pond Pudding

4oz butter
4oz demerara sugar
8oz self raising flour

4oz suet
1 lemon
A pinch of salt

Sieve the flour and salt into a mixing bowl and then stir in the suet. Mix with some cold water to form a soft but not sticky dough. Turn this out onto a floured surface and then knead until it is smooth. Reserve a third of the pastry for the lid and roll out the remainder and use it to line a pudding basin. Place half the sugar in the basin. Cut half the butter into small cubes and put these on top of the sugar. Prick the lemon with a fork and place it in the bowl. Now sprinkle the rest of the sugar over it and add the remaining butter, again cut into small cubes. Roll out the reserved pastry into a circle to form a lid. Dampen the edges of the pastry in the basin and then place the pastry lid on top. Trim the edges of the lid and seal the join firmly. Cover with a double sheet of foil pleated in the middle to allow for expansion. Steam for 3¼ hours. Turn the pudding out and serve, making sure that each person gets a portion of the lemon, which will have softened and burst during the cooking to form a sauce. Ann usually cooks this in a pressure cooker by putting 1½ pints of boiling water in the cooker and steaming the pudding for 35 minutes. She then cooks it at a lower pressure for a further 30 minutes, reducing the pressure slowly. We usually serve this with cream to make a delicious, rich dessert.

I learned so much from Pat during the 9 months that I worked with her that provided solid foundations for my subsequent career in the Probation Service. Often during those 33 years I would think about something Pat had told me or showed me that was relevant to the supervision of one or other of my probationers. She was an inspirational teacher and a wonderful friend and she exemplified the virtues of sincerity, commitment and fairness in everything that she did. She lived life to the full and died far too young. Her packed funeral in 1986 was the first time I had encountered a Humanist ceremony. I was so impressed with the way in which it was conducted, and the true celebration of Pat's life that it represented, that afterwards I made enquiries about humanism and the British Humanist Association, and I am now a Life member.

23

Holiday Romance

Not a topic one might expect to find in a book of reflections and reminiscences written by someone in their fifties but I wanted to write about one particular holiday romance and its influence on my life. The protagonist is not me but Ann, and the romance occurred long before I met her. After the breakdown of her first marriage Ann spent a few holidays going abroad on packages with a female friend. This provided not only sun and relaxation but also a break from single-handedly looking after her two daughters, who would stay with Auntie Hilda in Dudley for two weeks. One year Ann and her friend went to Sicily and there her dark 'gypsy' looks attracted the attention of one Giuseppe. He was a young handsome Sicilian whose wealthy family owned a large tile factory. Giuseppe's future wife had already been selected by them and he was open in telling Ann this, and in revealing that he was not particularly pleased about the plan. Thus a 'holiday romance' ensued for the fortnight of Ann's stay, at the end of which fond farewells were said at the airport and Ann returned to Dudley and her children and her part time job as a delivery driver, driving from shop to shop in the Potteries three days a week.

Apart from happy memories Ann also brought back with her from Sicily an interest in Italian food. This was perhaps one of the early influences that sparked her enthusiasm for exploring different cuisines. Recipes based on Italian cooking have become favourites in our household over the years, and none more so than Ann's version of the classic Italian meatloaf.

Sicilian Meatloaf

1lb minced beef or lamb
1 red onion
4oz chorizo sausage
2 garlic cloves, peeled and crushed
4 tablespoons parsley
1 egg
4 tomatoes, peeled and de-seeded
Salt and pepper
Olive oil

For the filling:
4oz pasta
3½oz cream cheese
1 tablespoon parsley
1 egg yolk
2oz blue cheese
For the topping:
1oz breadcrumbs
1oz parmesan cheese
1 tablespoon parsley

Take a 10 inch loaf tin, line it with foil and grease it with some olive oil. Preheat the oven to 180°C. Dice the sausage and the onion and dice and drain the tomatoes. Mix together the minced meat, sausage, onion, garlic, parsley, egg and tomatoes and season well. It is best to use a food processor to make this mixture because it needs to be as smooth and malleable as possible. Line the bottom and sides of the loaf tin with the mixture, leaving some left over. Now cook the pasta and drain it and while it is still hot add the cream cheese, egg yolk and parsley. Put this mixture in the meat lined tin and then cover this with the remaining meat mixture. Fold the foil over the top and bake in the oven for an hour. Remove from the oven and turn the meatloaf out onto a baking tray. You may need to drain off any liquid that comes out of the loaf at this stage. Mix the Parmesan, parsley and breadcrumbs together and sprinkle this mixture over the top of the meatloaf. Bake for a further 15 minutes.

Whenever we serve this dish at a dinner party it is inevitable that sooner or later someone will ask Ann about when she first encountered Italian cooking. She will then tell the tale of her holiday in Sicily. The account of her holiday romance with Giuseppe usually interests our guests, but it is when she goes on to explain the sequel that she really grabs everyone's attention.

For Ann the happy memories of her two weeks with Giuseppe sufficed, but this was clearly not the situation as far as he was concerned. Some months after her return to Dudley, in the depths of the winter and after the memories of her Sicilian holiday (and romance) had almost faded away to nothing, there was an unexpected knock on her door one Saturday afternoon. Ann opened the door and there on the doorstep was Giuseppe.

After recovering her composure she asked him in and he explained that he was on a visit to London and had so wanted to see her again that he had hired a taxi there and told the driver to take him to her address in Dudley. The taxi waited outside her small terraced house for two hours while Giuseppe tried to persuade her to go back to Sicily with him. Eventually he had to acknowledge that she wasn't going to accept his offer and he set off back to London in his taxi, this time never to be seen by her again.

So the attractions of Sicilian sun, sea, sex and money were not enough to turn her head and some years later she ended up with me, and we ended up here in Broncroft, and eventually I ended up writing this book, and none of that would have happened if Giuseppe's astonishingly romantic proposal had been accepted by her.

24
At The End

So here we are at the end of these reminiscences and you've almost got to the main recipe section, **Mainly Recipes**. Perhaps you've already read that, or fast forwarded to particular chapters when a recipe in the text has prompted your interest. Maybe these are the first words of the book that you've read, and you're wondering what on earth it can all be about.

My hope is that the apparently random nature of this book has/will make some sense for you, in whatever way you choose to read it. In the 1960s the novelist B.S.Johnson published his novel *The Unfortunates* as a set of separately bound chapters in a box, the idea being that the reader could, indeed had to, read them in whatever order he chose. This was intended by Johnson to reflect the random nature of thoughts and events as they crowd in upon us, one thought or event leading to another and back again, with any one 'order' being as valid as any other. I haven't consciously tried to imitate Johnson here, but I have intended that these pieces of prose can be read in whatever order the reader chooses. Ann's superb home cooking is what sparked all this in the first place and so the recipes are intended to be the main course. But like a Greek meal, the order in which you consume the various dishes on offer is entirely up to you. But please do try some of the recipes out and enjoy eating (or maybe drinking) the results. And if you've enjoyed reading some of what I've written to complement the recipes then so much the better.

Mainly Recipes

25

Drinks

Elderflower Cordial

20 large heads of elderflower
2¼ lb granulated sugar
1 lb light soft brown sugar
2 lemons finely sliced

2 oz tartaric acid (or citric acid if tartaric
is not available)
2¼ pints boiling water

Try to pick the elderflower heads when they are really well out and the pollen is visible on the flowers. Take the heads off the stalks, removing as much of the green as possible. Put in a large, wide bowl. Add the lemon slices and the tartaric acid. Pour on the boiling water and stir well. Now add the sugars and stir vigorously again. Cover and leave but stir 2 or 3 times a day for the next 5 days. Strain the liquid through muslin and bottle.

Although we generally make wine with the natural ingredients we harvest from trees and hedgerows, this is a delicious non alcoholic beverage that we make every year. We got this recipe from our neighbouring farmer's wife so we regard it as a real south Shropshire country recipe. It is vital that you do not allow anything metal near the cordial so make sure you only use wooden spoons! We usually dilute this cordial with sparkling water to make a lovely refreshing summer drink.

See also: Dandelion Wine (p57); Oak Leaf Wine (p58); Damson Wine (p59).

26

Soups

Carrot, Apple And Cashew Nut Soup

1 lb carrots
1 large onion
1 small potato
1 large cooking apple

2 oz butter
2 pints vegetable stock
2 oz broken cashew nuts
Salt and pepper

Chop the vegetables and the apple. Melt the butter in a pan and sauté this mixture for 5 minutes. Add the remaining ingredients, bring to the boil, cover and simmer for 30 minutes. Allow to cool and then whizz it in a food processor until the consistency is smooth. These quantities will serve six.

Green Pea And Mint Soup

1¼ lb frozen peas
1 teaspoon mint
1½ pints chicken stock

1 chopped onion
2 oz butter
Double cream to decorate

Place the peas, mint, chicken stock and onion in a large saucepan. Bring to the boil and then simmer gently for 20 minutes. Liquidise in a blender with the butter. Serve either hot or cold with a swirl of cream.

For reliability and ease we always go for *Green Pea And Mint Soup*. There are always frozen peas in the freezer and a few sprigs of mint in the garden, and we've also had success with an Irish recipe for soup made from swede.

Swede Soup

14 oz peeled and grated swedes
8 oz peeled and grated onions
2 oz butter
1 level tablespoon corn flour
1 pint chicken stock

¼ pint milk
4 tablespoons cream
Chopped parsley
Salt and pepper

This is Ann's own recipe devised in an attempt to replicate a wonderful swede soup we ate in a tiny restaurant in Clifden on the west coast of Ireland in 1994. It is unusual in that the raw swede is grated. Melt the butter in a saucepan, gently fry the swedes and onion in it for 10 minutes, and then remove from the heat. Mix the corn flour in a little cold water. Add this to the vegetables, together with the stock and seasoning, and simmer for a further 20 minutes. Then add the milk and cream and mix in. Serve into bowls and sprinkle the parsley on top.

Alice's Soup

4 oz Cambozola cheese
1 medium size potato
4 courgettes

¾ pint chicken stock
Fresh or dried basil
½ pint milk

Dice the courgettes and potato and fry them in butter. Add the chicken stock and simmer until tender. Liquidise with the cheese and basil and thin with the milk. Season to taste.. This recipe is from a local farmer's wife.

See also: Artichoke Soup (p36); Spinach Soup (p37); Creamy Potato And Onion Soup (p40); Lentil Coconut And Lime Soup (p65); Chicken Soup (p88).

V R POST OFFICE

Last Collection Time
Monday to Friday
11.00am
A later collection is made at
6.00pm from the Postbox at
Clovan Arms Delivery Office
King Lane Industrial Estate

Saturday
7.45am

Other Collections
Additional collections may be made
throughout the day until the Box Office
closes

27

Salads

Most salads that we eat are quickly constructed with the leaves and other ingredients that happen to be to hand. Here are two more formal recipes that make interesting and unusual salads. Both of them are also good for parties as the quantities make a good size dish of salad.

Mild Onion Salad

2 large red onions
The juice of 3 lemons
2 teaspoons sugar

1 large cucumber
Salt and pepper
4 tomatoes

Peel the onions, slice them thinly, and then put them in a bowl. Add 6 tablespoons of lemon juice and the sugar and mix it all together well. Now cover the bowl and leave for at least 12 hours. Peel and slice the cucumber thinly. Put it in a bowl, sprinkle with salt and leave for one hour. Slice the tomatoes thinly and put them in a salad bowl. Squeeze the liquid out of the onion and cucumber and add to the bowl. This is the core of the salad. You can now add anything else that takes your fancy. We have used peppers; lettuce; water cress; artichokes; basil leaves; green beans and feta cheese in various combinations. Just before serving toss with olive oil and the remaining lemon juice and season to taste. The beauty of this salad is that it is suitable for people like me who don't like raw onion.

Puy Lentil Salad

12 oz puy lentils
2 bay leaves
7 oz fresh tomatoes
2 small, diced red onions
2 tablespoons pumpkin seeds
Salt and pepper

For the dressing:
1 crushed clove of garlic
3 floz white wine vinegar
5 floz olive oil

Cover the lentils and bay leaves with water. Bring to the boil and simmer for 20 minutes. Dry roast the pumpkin seeds. Make the dressing by mixing the olive oil with the crushed garlic and whisking in the white wine vinegar. (Alternatively, put the garlic, vinegar and olive oil in a jar and shake furiously). Drain the lentils and place them in a bowl. Mix in the red onions, dressing and the tomatoes. Season to taste. (It is important not to put salt in with the lentils when you are cooking them as this will make them tough.)

Vegetarian

Vegetable Crumble

For the base:
1 carrot
A few sticks of celery
1 small swede
1 leek
A few peas
8 oz tin of tomatoes
1 large onion
3 tablespoons parsley
¼ pint milk
½ pint stock

2 oz butter
1 oz flour
Salt and pepper

For the topping:
6 oz brown flour
3 – 4 oz butter
4 oz grated cheese
2 oz chopped mixed nuts
2 tablespoons sesame seeds

Preheat the oven to 190°C. First make the base by cleaning, peeling and chopping the vegetables. Fry the onion in butter in a saucepan until pale brown. Add the rest of the vegetables except the tomatoes and cook gently for ten minutes, stirring occasionally. Now mix in the flour and gradually add the liquids and tomatoes while stirring. Add the parsley, salt and pepper and simmer gently for fifteen minutes. Place in a casserole and leave to stand. Now make the topping by rubbing the butter into the flour. Add the cheese, nuts and sesame seeds. Sprinkle the topping on top of the vegetables and bake for about 30 minutes until light brown in colour.

Pizza Base And Topping

For the base:
8 oz self raising or whole-wheat flour
2 oz margarine or butter
A pinch of salt
¼ pint fresh milk or yoghurt
Herbs to taste
Salt and pepper

For the topping:
1 tin of tomatoes
A pinch of herbs
Salt and pepper
Garlic
3 oz cheese

Rub the margarine or butter into the sieved flour and salt. Add herbs and pepper to taste. Add enough milk or yoghurt to give a light spongy dough just firm enough to handle. Turn onto a floured surface and knead very lightly to remove cracks. Roll out into a circle about the size of a dinner plate. Put on a baking tray. Boil the tomatoes, herbs, garlic, salt and pepper together until fairly thick and the juice has evaporated. Cool the mixture and then place on top of the pizza base. Grate the cheese and sprinkle it over the top and then cook for 15 minutes in a hot oven.

Aubergines With Pasta And Cheese (Served With French Cauliflower)

2 medium size aubergines
Olive oil
8 oz pasta shapes
8 oz strong grated cheese

½ pint tomato sauce made with 3 tablespoons tomato purée and water
1 crushed clove of garlic
Salt and pepper

Preheat the oven to 180C. Cut the aubergines into thin slices and cook them in olive oil until they are soft and slightly brown. Cook the pasta 'al dente'. Put layers in a baking dish of the tomato sauce, aubergines, pasta, cheese, seasoning and garlic. Finish with a layer of the cheese. Bake for 25 minutes.

Ann's current 'pasta of choice' for this dish is casarecce. Usually we serve this with *French Cauliflower* (please find that recipe on p167 and photograph on p164) but it goes just as well with a green salad if that is preferred. It's a dish that makes non-vegetarians envious when we have a 'mixed' dinner party.

French Cauliflower

1 lb cauliflower florets
1 oz pumpkin seeds

Mustard and cress
4 tablespoons French dressing

Cook cauliflower in boiling water for 1 minute, then drain and leave to cool. Place in a bowl with the other ingredients.

Rice And Vegetable Bake

For the base:
1 oz butter
1 small onion finely chopped
6 oz basmati rice
12 floz vegetable stock
1 egg lightly beaten
Salt and pepper

For the filling:
1 oz butter
1 leek sliced
1 crushed garlic cubes
6 oz thinly sliced courgettes

1 diced red pepper
8 oz chopped tomatoes
Salt and pepper

For the topping:
1 oz butter
1 oz wholemeal flour
9 floz milk
5 oz grated Cheddar cheese
1 egg lightly beaten
¼ teaspoon ground nutmeg
Salt and pepper

Preheat the oven to 190°C. Make the base by melting the butter in a pan, adding the onion and cooking until transparent. Now add the rice and stock. Bring to the boil then cover and simmer for 25 minutes. Allow to cool then stir in the egg. Season and press the rice mixture over the base of a well greased 9 inch square ovenproof dish. Now make the filling by melting the butter in a frying pan. Add the leek and garlic and cook for a minute. Then add the courgettes and pepper and cook for a further minute. Add the tomato and continue to cook until the vegetables are just tender (about 5 minutes). Season and arrange over the rice base. To make the topping melt the butter in a pan. Stir in the flour and cook over a gentle heat for 1 minute. Add the milk and stir until the sauce boils and thickens. Remove from the heat. Stir in half the cheese. Allow to cool slightly. Now add the egg, nutmeg, salt and pepper. Pour the mixture over the vegetable filling and top with the remaining cheese. Bake in the oven for 25 to 30 minutes until golden. These quantities serve 6.

Mediterranean Tartlets

For the pastry:
8oz plain flour
4oz butter
2oz vegetable fat
A pinch of salt
1 egg yolk
2 tablespoons cold water

For the filling:
1 clove garlic
2oz feta cheese
3 tablespoons mayonnaise
½ courgette grated
5 olives chopped
½ red pepper
½ red onion
2 tablespoons tomato paste

Preheat the oven to 190°C. Make the pastry by sifting the dry ingredients together. Place them in a bowl and make a well in the centre. Squeeze the fats together through your hands and soften them into walnut size lumps. Place these in the well and add the egg yolk and water. Knead the mixture together until smooth, shape it into small balls and place them in the mini muffin pan. Shape into tartlets using a dibber or your fingers and thumbs. Put all the ingredients for the filling into a bowl and mix them together. Put the mixture in the tartlet shells and bake in the oven for 10 minutes.

Vegetable Risotto With Basil

A small tub of fresh pesto
2½ oz parmesan cheese
Extra virgin olive oil
7 oz carrots
8 spring onions
4 oz fine green beans
5 oz radishes

4 oz mange tout
1 large onion
2 large garlic cloves
11½ oz risotto rice
5 floz dry white wine
2½ oz mascarpone cheese
Salt and pepper

Peel and cut the carrots into ¾ inch chunks. Trim the spring onions and cut in half. Top the beans but leave the tails. Halve the radishes. Bring a saucepan of water to the boil. Add the carrots and cook for 3 minutes, then add the radishes and cook for a further 2 minutes. Now add all the green vegetables and cook for another 2 minutes. Drain the vegetables and keep the cooking water for the risotto. Put the vegetables into a bowl of iced water. When they are cold, drain them. Cook the onion and garlic in 2 tablespoons of olive oil for 5 minutes. Stir in the rice and cook without letting it brown for 2 minutes. Add the wine and boil until it has evaporated. Add 1¼ pints of warm cooking water and bring to the boil. Simmer for 18 minutes, adding more warm liquid as necessary. After the risotto has cooked for 14 minutes heat 4 floz of water in a pan, add the vegetables and heat through until the water has evaporated. Add 1 tablespoon of olive oil and season well. Once the risotto is cooked remove from the heat and stir in the mascarpone and the pesto. Sprinkle the parmesan cheese over the finished dish before serving.

Aubergines Stuffed With Cheese

4 aubergines (about 1½ lb in total)
1 onion, finely chopped
6 oz grated Cheddar cheese

1 egg
1 tablespoon parsley
Salt and pepper

Set the oven to 200°C. Boil the aubergines in a half full saucepan of salted water for 5 minutes or until they are barely tender. Drain and cool the aubergines and then split them in half lengthways. Scoop the flesh out leaving the skins intact and then arrange the skins in a greased shallow ovenproof dish. Mash the aubergine flesh with a fork then stir in the grated onion and cheese, the egg, the parsley and salt and pepper. Fill the skins with the mixture and bake for 30 to 40 minutes until they are golden brown.

These quantities will serve 4. Serve with a salad. This dish is Balkan in origin.

Cauliflower Moussaka

1 cauliflower in florets
½ pint milk
Salt and pepper
12oz sliced aubergines
Olive oil
For the tomato sauce:
1lb skinned and chopped tomatoes, or a
   can of tomatoes
2 chopped celery sticks

1 chopped onion
2 cloves of garlic
1 teaspoon dried oregano
1 tablespoon tomato purée
For the cheese sauce:
1½oz butter
1oz plain flour
2 eggs
2oz Cheddar cheese

Preheat the oven to 180°C. Poach the cauliflower in milk for 5 minutes. Drain, reserve the milk and make it up to ½ pint with water. Chop the cauliflower finely and season well. Simmer the ingredients for the tomato sauce in a covered pan for 15 minutes, stirring occasionally until thick. Make the cheese sauce, cool for 5 minutes then add the eggs and cheese and season well. Brown the aubergine slices. Mix half the cheese sauce with the cauliflower. Grease a deep 3 pint baking dish. Start layering this with aubergines, cauliflower mixture and then tomato sauce. Finish with a layer of aubergines. Cover with the remaining cheese sauce and cook in the oven for 30 minutes.

Stuffed Tomatoes

4 large firm tomatoes
3 potatoes
1oz basil
1 clove of garlic
4 tablespoons olive oil

3½oz plus 2 extra tablespoons of grated
   parmesan cheese
3 eggs
Salt and pepper

Preheat the oven to 200°C. Cut the tomatoes in half. With a spoon scoop out the seeds and pulp. (You can keep these for a stew). Sprinkle the tomatoes very lightly with salt and turn them upside down to let the juices come out. Peel the potatoes and boil until tender. Drain and mash them. Add the basil, garlic, 3½oz of cheese, salt, pepper, and 2 tablespoons of oil and mix well. Add the eggs and beat with a fork until they have been absorbed. Stuff the tomato halves with this mixture and place on an oiled baking dish. Drizzle some oil over the tomatoes and sprinkle them with the 2 extra tablespoons of cheese. Bake for 30 to 45 minutes until the tomatoes have softened. Be careful not to let them fall apart.

Even though neither of us is vegetarian we now have a substantial number of vegetarian recipes that Ann has built up over the years to cater for those of our friends and family who are. Sometimes when we have a 'mixed' group of dinner guests, the vegetarian option is so enticing that the carnivores have to be prevented from eating it all themselves. The recipes for *Vegetable Crumble* (p165) and *Aubergines With Pasta And Cheese* (p166) definitely fall into that category. Here is another delicious vegetarian dish that the carnivores round the dinner table are likely to steal unless they are carefully watched..

Carrot And Coriander Roulade

2oz butter
1lb grated carrots
4 eggs, separated
1 tablespoon chopped coriander leaves

For the filling:
6oz soft cheese flavoured with garlic
  and herbs
1 tablespoon chopped coriander leaves
2 or 3 tablespoons crème fraiche

Preheat the oven to 200°C. Line a 12 inch by 8 inch Swiss roll tin with parchment. Melt the butter, add the carrots and cook for 5 minutes. Transfer to a bowl and allow to cool. Now add the egg yolk and coriander and season and mix together. Whisk the egg whites to firm peaks and then stir in 2 tablespoons of the carrot mixture. Fold in the rest of the carrot mixture. Spread the mixture in a tin and bake for 10 to 15 minutes until it has risen and is firm to the touch. Turn it out onto parchment paper, cover with a clean damp cloth and allow to cool. Make the filling by putting the soft cheese in a bowl. Mix in the coriander and enough crème fraiche to yield a spreading consistency. Spread this mixture on the roulade leaving a ½ inch border all round. Roll it up from the short side using the paper to help with this process and cut into slices to serve.

See also: Courgette Fritters (p46); Chestnut And Vegetable Hotpot (p66); Cheddar Cheese And Onion Pie (p86); George Bernard Shaw's Cheese And Celery Pie (p87); Rich Three Cheese Pie (p100).

D.W.W...

Ludlow Amateur Boxing Club
SHOW TIME

Ludlow Race...
Friday 21st O...
from 6.30pm...

TABLE PRICE:...

GAME NOW ALAILABLE

TRADITIONAL
BREEDS
MEAT MARKETING

D.W. WALL & SON
High Class Family
BUTCHERS

2011 LUDLOW FESTIVAL SAUSAGE WINNERS

LOCAL FREE RANGE Pork

PEOPLE CHOICE AND PROFESSIONAL CHOICE

REG MAY & SONS

HAND RAISED
PORK PIES

WINNER OF LUDLOW FOOD
FESTIVAL 2011

AVAILABLE HERE

HIGH CLASS

LOCAL
Rare Breed Pork
From G. Williams
Leintwardine

D.W. WALL & SON
Home of the
Award Winning
Ludlow Sausage
And many

Meat

Greek Country Sausages

1 teaspoon dried thyme
½ teaspoon ground allspice
1 teaspoon ground coriander
1 ground bay leaf
2 lb lean pork finely diced
8 oz streaky bacon
1 tablespoon cracked black pepper
Salt

The zest of an orange
4 tablespoons toasted pine nuts
  coarsely ground
1 oz fresh wholemeal breadcrumbs
1 crushed clove of garlic
3 tablespoons chopped parsley
3 floz red wine
Olive oil

First of all make a mixture of the spices by mixing together the thyme, allspice, coriander and bay leaf. You can do this using a traditional mortar and pestle, or just use a bowl and the end of a rolling pin. Put all the other ingredients, except the olive oil and wine, in a bowl and mix them together. Add the spice mixture and then add enough wine to make the mixture moist so that it sticks together. Cover the bowl and leave it for 30 minutes to allow the flavours to mingle. Dust a surface with some flour and then divide the mixture into about 12 portions and roll each one out in the flour to make a sausage shape about 4 or 5 inches long. Heat 4 tablespoons of olive oil in a frying pan and fry the sausages over a low/medium heat, turning them occasionally, until they are golden brown. Serve with lemon wedges and sprinkle with parsley. This recipe is adapted from Rosemary Barron's book 'Flavours of Greece', given to Ann as a present by Mark and Helen..

Pheasant And Beef Casserole

1 pheasant cleaned and dressed
1 lb stewing beef
2 large onions
2 tablespoons flour
¼ pint red wine
¾ pint beef stock

1 tablespoon red wine vinegar
½ teaspoon thyme
4 tablespoons cranberry sauce
4 oz mushrooms (optional)
Salt and pepper

Preheat the oven to 160°C. Coat the stewing beef in flour, leave the pheasant whole and dust with flour, then seal both and put them in a casserole dish. Lightly fry the onions and then stir in the wine, stock and vinegar and bring to the boil. Season to taste and add the thyme and cranberry sauce. Pour over the beef and pheasant, cover, and cook for 2 hours. If you are using mushrooms add them to the casserole 30 minutes before the end of the cooking time. This is a recipe from Liz and Garry who farm the land all around our house. Ann doesn't eat pheasant so this recipe is especially useful as it enables her to put the pheasants that we are sometimes given by shooting friends to good use. When she serves it she gives me all the pheasant and has the beef for herself!

We now buy almost all our meat from D.W.Wall in Ludlow, including the smoked bacon for my golfer's breakfast (see p93). They also supply us with the best sausages in the world, made to the secret recipe originated by former Ludlow butchers, Carters and, as the shop window in the photograph on p172 proclaims, the winner of both sausage categories at the 2011 Ludlow Food Festival. Shame about the solitary hare hanging up there though (see pp35-36).

Ann's Steak Pie

For the filling:
1½ lb stewing steak
8oz onions, peeled and chopped
3 tablespoons white flour
1 pint beef stock
1 tablespoon Worcester sauce
1 teaspoon dried thyme

3 tablespoons olive oil
Salt and pepper
For the pastry:
12oz self raising flour
6oz suet
Salt and pepper

Preheat the oven to 140°C. Fry the steak in batches in olive oil in an oven proof casserole dish. Ann uses a le Creuset dish. As each portion is done remove it and put it aside on a plate. When all the meat is browned lightly fry the onion in the casserole dish. Now take it off the heat and stir in the flour, stock, herbs, Worcester sauce and seasoning. Put it back on the heat and bring it to the boil, then add the steak. Cover the casserole and cook in the oven for 2 hours or until the meat is tender. Remove from the oven and leave it to cool and then put it in a pie dish. The pie crust can be made from short crust or puff pastry but my favourite is suet pastry. Preheat the oven to 220°C. Sift the flour into a bowl. Mix in the suet and some salt with your hands or a fork. Add water a little at a time as you are mixing, adding just enough to bind the mixture. Now roll the pastry out thickly and fit it over the pie dish. Crimp the edges and put a slit in the top to let the air out as it cooks. Cook in the oven for 30–40 minutes or until the pastry is browned on top.

Obviously I am biased, but I truly believe that this is the best steak pie I have ever tasted.

See also: Turkish Lamb Casserole (p23); Pastitsio (p48); Mrs Finn's Curry (p105); Beef And Beer Curry (p117); Alistair's Spare Ribs (p139); Sicilian Meatloaf (p148).

Chicken, Ginger And Apple Curry

3 chicken breasts
1 oz butter
2 tablespoons olive oil
1 large onion
Curry paste to taste
1 oz flour
¾ pint chicken stock

1 large apple
Small piece of root ginger
1 tablespoon mango chutney
1 teaspoon brown sugar
1 bay leaf
2 tablespoons Greek yoghurt
1 teaspoon lemon juice

Preheat the oven to 180°C. Heat the butter and oil in a pan and fry the chicken until it is golden brown. Transfer to a casserole dish. Fry the chopped onion in the remaining fat for 5 minutes. Add the curry paste and fry over a low heat for another 5 minutes, stirring occasionally. Stir in the flour and then gradually blend in the stock. Add the peeled and chopped apple, chutney, sugar, grated ginger, bay leaf and salt and pepper. Stir well and bring back to the boil and then pour over the chicken. Cook in the oven for 45 to 60 minutes. When cooked stir in the yoghurt and lemon juice. Heat gently through. Serve with rice.

Although our 'standard' curry dish is *Mrs Finn's Curry* (see p105), Ann always follows this recipe in the days following Christmas Day, using left over turkey breast instead of chicken. We still adhere to Mrs Finn's insistence on only using Fern's mild curry paste though.

As I've already mentioned in Chapter 17, Ann often makes a chicken dish when we have guests for dinner. This next recipe is one of our favourites.

Cooper's Chicken

2 tablespoons olive oil
3 medium sized leeks (about 1¾lb), trimmed and sliced
5 floz dandelion wine (or dry sherry)
7 floz chicken stock
14 floz crème fraiche
2 level teaspoons plain flour
2 level tablespoons whole grain mustard
3 level teaspoons sage

1 level teaspoon parsley
1½ lb chicken breast cut into ½ inch strips
3½ oz Gruyère cheese, grated

For the topping:
2½ oz breadcrumbs
3 tablespoons olive oil
2½ oz smoked bacon, chopped
2 level tablespoons chopped parsley

Fry the leeks over a gentle heat until softened. Remove and set aside. Add the dandelion wine and stock, bring to the boil, and bubble until reduced by a quarter. Allow to cool. Preheat the oven to 190°C. Mix the crème fraiche, flour, mustard, sage and parsley together with salt and pepper, then mix in the stock, the leeks and the pieces of chicken. Pour this mixture into a 4 pint oven proof dish and sprinkle the cheese on top. Put the breadcrumbs into a bowl with the olive oil, bacon and parsley. Mix these together and sprinkle them over the chicken. Cook in the oven for 50 to 60 minutes. If it gets too brown cover lightly with foil. Ann got this fabulous chicken recipe from some friends who live further down the Dale and she has used it to great effect on several occasions since then.

Chicken With Garlic Sauce

1 oz butter
2 tablespoons olive oil
6 pieces of chicken (8oz each)
6 cloves of garlic
¼ pint white wine
6 tablespoons balsamic or red wine vinegar

1 tablespoon tomato purée
1 teaspoon Dijon mustard
Salt and pepper
½ pint double cream
1 oz toasted pine nuts
1 oz sultanas

Melt the butter and oil in a heavy based pan. Add the chicken and cook over a high heat for a few minutes until brown on both sides. Add the unpeeled garlic. Reduce the heat, cover and cook for 30 to 35 minutes until the chicken is tender. Remove the chicken and keep warm in a low oven covered with foil. Add the wine, vinegar, puree and mustard to the garlic in the pan and season well. Bring to the boil, reduce the heat and simmer until the liquid is thick and syrupy, stirring and scraping the bottom of the pan as you do this. Pour all of the liquid and garlic through a sieve and using the back of a spoon press the garlic cloves so they release the softened garlic into the sauce. Place the cream in a pan and heat until slightly thickened, then stir in the garlic sauce until it is well mixed. Pour the sauce over the hot chicken and sprinkle with nuts and sultanas.

Chicken Supreme With Mango, Ginger And Coriander

6 chicken breasts skinned and boned
2 tablespoons olive oil
1 oz butter
2 floz white wine or chicken stock
1 mango peeled and chopped

1 inch piece of fresh ginger grated
1 tablespoon fresh coriander
10 floz double cream
Flour and seasoning

Preheat the oven to 180°C. Dust the chicken with flour and seasoning. Heat the oil and butter together in a frying pan. Cook the chicken in the hot fat for 15 to 20 minutes until it is golden on all sides and just cooked through. Transfer the chicken to an oven proof casserole dish. Pour the stock or wine around the chicken and cook covered in the hot oven for 10 minutes while preparing the sauce. Cook the mango in the fat that is left in the pan for 2 minutes. Stir in the ginger and coriander and cook for another minute. Stir in the cream, season to taste and cook until the sauce is slightly thickened. Pour the sauce onto your dinner plates and place a chicken breast on top. Garnish with sprigs of coriander. Serve with rice or new potatoes.

Cretan Chicken Pie (Tzoulamas)

1 chicken (5–6lb) cut into serving pieces
  and skin and fat removed
1 large chopped onion
2 carrots, scrubbed and cut into thick
  slices
1 large bunch of parsley
Chicken stock
Salt and pepper
5 tablespoons olive oil
4 shallots finely chopped
1 tablespoon ground cumin
8oz long grain rice

6 bay leaves
Juice of 2 lemons
Finely grated zest of 1 lemon
1 large clove of garlic finely chopped
4 tablespoons of capers, rinsed
1lb filo pastry
8oz butter
2oz grated feta cheese
12oz cottage cheese, drained
7oz raisins
4oz lightly toasted pine nuts

Place the chicken pieces, onion, carrot, and stock in a large saucepan. Season with salt and pepper and bring slowly to the boil. Cover, reduce the heat and simmer for 40 minutes or until the chicken is cooked. Strain over a bowl. Set aside 16 fl oz of the liquid. Discard the vegetables. Warm 4 tablespoons of oil in a saucepan and sauté the shallots for 10 minutes. Add the cumin and cook for a further minute. Stir in the rice, reserved stock, bay leaves and salt to taste and bring to a boil without stirring. Cook uncovered for 8 minutes or until the liquid has evaporated. Remove from the heat, cover with a lid and set aside for 30 minutes. Remove the chicken from the bones and cut the meat into small pieces. Place the chicken in a bowl and sprinkle with half the lemon juice and pepper to taste. Set aside 2 tablespoons of parsley and add all but 1 tablespoon of the lemon zest, the garlic, 3 tablespoons of the capers and a pinch of salt to the remaining parsley. Chop to mix. Combine with the chicken making sure each piece is coated. Cover and set aside. Heat the oven to 190°C. Mash the feta and cottage cheese together using a fork. Melt 6 ozs of butter over a low heat and add the remaining olive oil. Divide the filo sheets into 2 portions and use one sheet to line a baking tray that you have brushed with the butter mixture. Repeat with the remaining sheets of that portion of the filo but do not brush the last sheet. Each time you add a sheet turn the tin 90 degrees. Spread the rice mixture over the filo and then spread with the chicken and parsley mixture. Scatter the cheese mixture evenly over the chicken, then sprinkle on the raisins and pine nuts. Sprinkle with a few tablespoons of the chicken stock. Fold the edges of the filo over the filling and brush with the butter mixture. From the second portion of filo lay one sheet over the filling letting the edges hang over the sides of the tin. Lightly brush with the butter mixture and layer until all the sheets are used. Do not butter the last sheet. Tuck the top filo sheets in around the bottom of the pie. Butter the top sheet and score the top two filo sheets into diamond shapes. Bake for 35–40 minutes or until deep golden brown.

While the pie is baking heat the remaining butter in a saucepan over low heat for 10 minutes. Add the remaining lemon juice and set aside. Chop the parsley and remaining capers and lemon zest together. When the pie is cooked cut through the score marks to the bottom of the tin. Put a large plate over the pie, turn upside down, remove the tin, put another plate over the pie and turn again so the pie is right side up. Make a hole in the centre of the pie and pour the brown butter into it and sprinkle the parsley mixture over the pie. Now it is ready to serve and eat!

This is a very complicated recipe, but it is a very special pie, traditionally forming the centrepiece of a Cretan village wedding feast. The recipe comes from Rosemary Barron's book, *Flavours Of Greece.*

Chicken With Tomatoes And Honey

3 whole chicken breasts on the bone
  split in two
2 chopped onions
6 cloves of garlic
1 cinnamon stick
½ teaspoon of ground ginger
A generous pinch of saffron
4½ lbs blanched and peeled ripe
  tomatoes
1 large tablespoon honey
The juice of a lemon
Salt and pepper

Brown the chicken in olive oil until it is golden. Remove from the pan. Now fry the onions in the pan until they are golden and soft. Add all the spices except for the saffron. Roughly chop the tomatoes and add these to the pan with salt and pepper. Cook over a fierce heat until the tomatoes collapse and then turn down the heat. Return the chicken to the pan and simmer gently for about an hour, until the meat is tender. Remove the chicken and place it in a warmed serving dish. Continue cooking the sauce, stirring frequently, until it thickens and the tomatoes begin to caramelise. Now crumble in the saffron threads and add the lemon juice and honey. Cook for another 5 minutes, stirring continuously. Check the seasoning and then pour the sauce over the chicken, and serve. An additional touch is to strew some roasted almonds and sesame seeds over the dish just before you serve. Ann's version of this dish is adapted from an original recipe by Claudia Roden.

See also: Greek Style Roast Chicken (p112); Coronation Chicken (p120).

181

Vegetables

A n inventive vegetable dish can transform a meal into something special and Winter Medley is good enough to eat on its own. It is one of my all time favourites and can be served hot, or alternatively put in the freezer and used at a later date. To do this allow it to cool and then over wrap with foil and seal, label and freeze. Use it within 3 months by thawing for 6 hours at room temperature and then cook covered for 45 minutes at 200°C.

Winter Medley

4 tablespoons olive oil
1 lb coarsely grated carrots
8 oz coarsely grated parsnips
8 oz coarsely grated swedes
8 oz sliced leeks

For the sauce:
2 oz butter or margarine
2 oz plain flour
1½ pints milk
6 oz grated mature Cheddar cheese
Salt and pepper
4 oz fresh brown breadcrumbs

Preheat the oven to 200°C. Heat the oil in a large pan. Add the carrots, parsnips, swedes and leeks. Lightly fry for ten minutes, stirring occasionally. Now make a white sauce and add the cheese and seasoning. Add the sauce to the cooked vegetables and mix well. Divide the mixture between three 2 pint gratin dishes (each one will serve four). Sprinkle the breadcrumbs over the dishes. Cook for 25 minutes.

Courgettes With Olive Oil And Herbs

To serve 4:
1½ lb sliced smallish courgettes
4 tablespoons olive oil
The juice of 1 lemon

Salt and pepper
4 tablespoons parsley or coriander
1 tablespoon dried oregano

Heat the oven to 180°C. Put the courgettes in a shallow dish. Pour over the olive oil and half the lemon juice and add 4 fl oz of hot water. Sprinkle with salt and pepper and bake uncovered for 10 minutes. Turn the oven down to 150°C and bake for another 40 minutes. Stir the courgettes in the cooking liquid during cooking to keep them moist. Sprinkle with lemon juice, parsley, oregano, olive oil and salt and pepper before serving. Can be served either warm or cold. This is an adaptation of another Greek recipe from Rosemary Barron.

Green Beans Braised With Tomatoes And Garlic

7 oz runner beans
4 tablespoons olive oil
1 small red onion

2 cloves of garlic
5 tomatoes
Salt and pepper

Bring a saucepan of water to the boil and blanch the beans for 7 minutes. Heat the oil in a frying pan. Add the onion and garlic and cook until translucent. Add the tomatoes, beans, salt and pepper. Cook over a moderate heat and add an occasional spoonful of water to stop it sticking. Keep adjusting the heat as you see fit until you have a thick sauce and the beans are tender.

This dish can be eaten hot or cold. We first encountered it in Sivota in Epirus, on the Greek mainland. For 3 years we had wonderful holidays in a villa called Villa Galini (galini means 'peace' in Greek). The top floor of the 3 storey building was used by the owners every weekend. They would arrive on Friday evening from their home in Ioannina, the provincial capital of Epirus, and on Saturdays they would tend the beautiful gardens, which were full of gorgeous shrubs and flowers. We liked to sit in the garden to read for some of each day and occasionally Chrisoula would bring us a small dish or drink as a gesture of friendship and hospitality. This was one such dish. Afterwards we looked out for it in the tavernas and some did serve it, but they were never as tasty as Chrisoula's.

Carrot And Cardamom Pilaff

½lb grated carrots
6oz rice
1½–2oz toasted almonds and pistachios
Seeds from 6–8 cardamom pods
2 shallots

The zest of 1 large orange
¾ pint stock
A little honey
Olive oil

Chop the shallots and soften them for 2 to 3 minutes in a little olive oil. Crush the cardamom seeds and stir into the pan. Add the rice and cook gently for 3 to 4 minutes, stirring now and then. Add the carrots, orange zest and plenty of pepper and stir constantly for 2 minutes. Pour on the hot stock, stir in a teaspoon of honey and a pinch of salt and bring to the boil. Cover the pan and leave to simmer for 18 minutes. Season and stir in the nuts just before serving.

A salad goes well with this. Romaine lettuce and orange is good as it uses up the orange flesh. These quantities serve 4 to 6 as an accompaniment to meat or 2 to 3 as a vegetarian main course.

See also: Gratin Dauphinoise (p22); Peter's Gratin (p22).

Auntie Hilda's Christmas Pudding

¾ lb breadcrumbs
½ lb raisins
½ lb currants
½ lb sultanas
½ lb suet
4 oz mixed chopped peel
1 grated carrot
½ lb soft brown sugar

1½ oz blanched chopped almonds
½ of the juice and grated rind of a
  lemon
½ teaspoon nutmeg
½ teaspoon salt
2 teaspoons mixed spice
4 large eggs
½ pint beer or stout

Stir all the ingredients together well until the mixture is of a dropping consistency. Add a little milk if necessary. Put the mixture into greased basins and tie down with greaseproof paper and foil. These quantities make 4 lbs of mixture. Boil for 6 to 8 hours or alternatively, if using a pressure cooker, steam for 15 minutes with 2 ¼ pints of water in the steamer and then cook at high pressure for 1 ¾ hours. (These are the times and quantities for a 1lb pudding). Take off the covers and allow the puddings to dry out well before covering with clean dry paper and putting to store in a cool place. Boil for a further 2 hours on the day that you eat them, or reheat in a pressure cooker at high pressure for 20 minutes in 2 ¼ pints of water.

Auntie Hilda lived across the road from Ann when she lived in Dudley. She was not a blood relation but had become a surrogate 'aunt' to Ann and her sister when they were growing up, and then later took on the same role for Ann's two children. She had no children of her own. Ann's mother was evicted from her rented accommodation in Dudley in 1943 when her landlord found out that she was pregnant (with Ann, conceived during one of her R.A.F. father's home leaves). This was apparently a relatively 'normal' occurrence in the 'good old days'. Ann's now homeless mother knocked on doors in the town asking for accommodation and Auntie Hilda took her in. When she went into labour with Ann, Auntie Hilda ran through the blacked out streets of Dudley to fetch the midwife. After the war she worked as a waitress, amongst other places at Edgbaston Cricket Ground, and she got Ann her first waitressing job. When we were planning our wedding Auntie was working as a waitress at Dudley Masonic Hall. She arranged for us to use it for our reception at a cheap rate and she and her waitress colleagues did all the food. Ann and I had to be interviewed by the committee before being allowed to hire the premises. Apparently a number of my left leaning friends were somewhat bemused when they received the wedding invitation to attend the ceremony at Dudley Register Office "and afterwards at The Masonic Hall"!

Foolproof Sweet Pastry

½lb flour
4oz butter
2oz vegetable fat
1 tablespoon caster sugar

A pinch of salt
1 egg yolk
2 tablespoons water

Sift the dry ingredients together. Place them in a bowl and make a well in the centre. Squeeze the fats together through your hands and soften them into walnut size lumps. Place these in the well and add the egg yolk and water. Knead the mixture together until smooth. Refrigerate in floured polythene bags until firm. Use as required. This is a recipe given to us by our neighbour which has always proved to be as described, i.e. foolproof!

Acknowledgements

I would like to thank all the people who have helped bring this book to fruition.

Many people, too many to name individually, offered encouragement and good wishes, in particular many former colleagues in West Mercia Probation Service when the project was little more than an idea.

The following individuals kindly agreed that material obtained from them or relating to them could be included: Liz Beazley; Annamarie and Graham Bellinger; Robin Benians; Dick Cooper; Christine Favier; Mick and Joan Finn; Mandy Fowler; Margaret Geary; Dorothy Hankinson; Alice Hughes; Paul and Cheryl Mantle; Peter Munday; Tamsin Osler; Alaister and Margaret Peacock; Nigel and Vicky Round; Barbara Stoddart; Mark and Helen Wadlow; Wyndham and Bronwen Williams; Liz Wright.

Claudia Roden's agent, David Higham, and Anne Dolamore of Grub Street Publishing gave me permission to include adapted versions of Claudia Roden and Rosemary Barron recipes and their generous and helpful attitude is much appreciated.

Josh Bird and Paul Eaton took dozens of photographs especially for this book and their creativity and skill has enhanced it immeasurably.

Just when I was about to give up on the whole project Katie Arber and Paul Eaton gave me the support and advice I needed. Paul took on the role of designer and has transformed my text into a visual feast, putting up with my nagging anxieties with phlegmatic good humour as he has done so. I am sincerely grateful to him for all his efforts.

My wife Ann's recipes are the heart of this book and without them it would not have been worth writing, and without her I would not have been able to write it.

Photo Credits

All of the photographs in this book have a personal connection to me. Many were shot in and around the Corvedale especially for the book; the remainder were sourced from our family photograph albums. We have made every reasonable effort to correctly identify the photographer for each image used, but if there are any errors or omissions please contact the publisher and we will be pleased to rectify them in future editions.

Josh Bird: cover and pages 8, 20, 24, 30, 58, 190, 213.

Paul Eaton: pages 6, 7, 10, 13, 14, 19, 29, 37 (right), 38, 49, 54, 59, 61, 62, 73, 81, 84 (right), 89, 90, 92, 95, 101, 102, 108, 111 (left, right), 113 (right), 116, 128, 133, 137, 145, 150, 152, 159, 163, 174, 178 (left, right), 197, 203, 210, 217, 219, 220.

Ann Hankinson: page 67.

Ian Hankinson: pages 16, 31 (left, right), 33, 34, 37 (left), 42, 45, 47, 50, 56, 68, 74, 76, 79 (left, right), 84 (left), 85, 93, 96, 99, 104, 113 (left), 114, 119, 122, 126, 134, 154, 156, 160, 162, 164, 168, 172, 176, 182, 184, 188, 191, 192, 194, 198, 202, 204, 208.

Bethany Howells: page 82.

Liz Wright: page 11.

Cannock Advertiser (c.1979, photographer unknown): page 65.

Watercolour on page 38, *Cabbage* by **Ann Hankinson**.